Best Recipes Under the Sun

Best Recipes Under the Sun

MARION KANE

A TOTEM BOOK
Toronto

First published 1987
by TOTEM BOOKS
a division of Collins Publishers
100 Lesmill Road, Don Mills, Ontario

Canadian Cataloguing in Publication Data

Kane, Marion
    Best recipes under the Sun

Recipes originally published in The Toronto Sun.
Includes index.
ISBN 0-00-217756-0

1. Cookery.   I. Title.
TX715.K35 1987   641.5   C87-094393-6

Illustrations: Frances Beaulieu
Editorial and design: Abraham Tanaka Associates

Printed and bound in Canada

CONTENTS

To Sandy and Esther, who endured one week of tofu dinners during six months of recipe testing for this book and hardly *complained when I only emerged from my basement office for meals during the last month of hard-core writing.*

To Sun *columnist Karen Boulton, who tested and contributed many of the recipes for this book.*

INTRODUCTION

There are at least two people who will be relieved and delighted to see a copy of *Best Recipes Under the Sun*. Both *Sun* columnist Karen Boulton and myself have spent many moons rifling through piles of newspaper clippings, reluctantly culling recipes, testing and re-testing dishes to bring you this collection of our food section's best. And the two hundred plus recipes that appear certainly come bearing a badge of excellence.

It should come as no surprise to me that so many of the recipes in this book are tops in their genre. After all, when you get almost two hundred entries in a butter tart recipe contest, narrow them down to the top ten to be judged by an expert panel and then pick the all-time favorite, you can be sure it's a winner. And all the contest winners and runner-up recipes published here, from the Dishiest Dip Contest-winning taco dip to the pear almond tart that won our Parlez-Vous Gourmet contest, are top-notch.

In addition to these wonderful contributions from *Sun* readers, we have mooched many a dazzling restaurant specialty. From Rhodes' luscious Chinese cashew chicken salad to the orange almond salad from the Magic Pan (our most requested recipe ever), these are among the best and most innovative dishes that this city—a forerunner in North American cuisine—has to offer.

But we haven't forgotten everybody's comfort favorites. You'll also find the very best bran muffins, a dreamy rice pudding, terrific tuna casserole and the most rib-hugging chili con carne you're likely to come across.

Then there are the desserts and cakes. Just try the chocolate espresso cheesecake from the now-defunct restaurant, Basie's, whose memory is sure to live on in this dark and sinfully rich creation. Or my mom's famous linzertorte, guaranteed to rate raves from all who try it.

Which brings me to my one pang of guilt about this book. Over the past four years as editor of the *Toronto Sun* food section, as I ate my way through weekly taste testings and innumerable rich and wonderful dishes, I also became a firm advocate of nutritious eating. My food philosophy now is to eat a royal breakfast, go easy on fats, eat plenty of fruit and vegetables and show discrimination when indulging in decadent sweets. The result for me has been a streamlined shape plus an abundance of energy.

This book reflects the schizophrenic eating trends of a world where a realization that low-fat foods are the name of the game co-exists uneasily with a rampant craving for ice cream and chocolate truffles.

My answer to this dichotomy? Well, even the most devoted nutrition buffs need a little decadence now and then. I suggest filling up on pasta with chicken and a crisp side salad, then cutting yourself a tiny slice of our incredible carrot cake. A little will go a long way.

So here's cooking at you. And I trust you'll agree that these are truly some of the best recipes under the Sun!

Marion Kane
Toronto, 1987

APPETIZERS AND SOUPS

HERNANDO'S GREAT GUACAMOLE

We adapted the recipe from Hernando's Hideaway—a Toronto Tex-Mex restaurant known for this chili-zapped dip and margaritas—to come up with this terrific guacamole. Super with drinks at a party or Grey Cup get-together, this is best made with the flavorful Haas avocados from Mexico, which are available almost year-round at specialty greengrocers. Don't be put off by the avocado's rough, darkish skin—a sign of perfect ripeness. And don't make this without the fresh coriander (also known as Chinese parsley or cilantro), which gives a wonderful flavor to the dip. Fresh coriander can be found in Chinese and specialty grocery stores.

1	ripe tomato	1
1 tbsp	seeded and finely chopped canned or fresh jalapeño peppers or to taste	15 mL
1	clove garlic, minced	1
3 tbsp	finely chopped onion	45 mL
1 tbsp	finely chopped fresh coriander	15 mL
2 tbsp	lemon or lime juice	25 mL
2	ripe Haas avocados, peeled, pitted and finely chopped	2
2 tbsp	sour cream or unflavored yogurt (optional)	25 mL
	Salt to taste	

• To peel tomato, cut an "X" in non-stem end and plunge into boiling water for 10 seconds. Peel off skin with sharp knife. To remove seeds, cut tomato in half horizontally and squeeze seeds gently from each half. Chop finely.

• Combine all ingredients in bowl. Mix well with fork. Cover with plastic wrap. Chill.

Serves 8 to 10 with crackers or tortilla chips for dipping.

LIME RICKEY'S TEX-MEX NACHOS

These fabulous nachos, loaded with chili con carne, cheese and jalapeño peppers, are all that this spicy Tex-Mex creation should be and more. The recipe comes from Cary Mausner of Lime Rickey's—a fifties diner in Thornhill, Ontario. Monterey Jack cheese gives an authentic flavor to nachos and is available in some supermarkets. Or you can use brick, mild white Cheddar, Swiss or any other light-colored, good-melting cheese.

1	210-g package round tortilla chips	1
2 cups	chili con carne, hot (page 87)	500 mL
1¼ cups	grated medium Cheddar cheese	300 mL
1¼ cups	grated Monterey Jack cheese	300 mL
1	large ripe tomato, diced	1
¼ cup	drained, seeded and chopped canned or fresh jalapeño peppers or to taste	50 mL
½ cup	sour cream or unflavored yogurt	125 mL

- Preheat broiler.
- Spread tortilla chips evenly on large ovenproof plate or baking pan. Top with chili. Sprinkle with cheeses. Broil until cheese melts. Do not brown.
- Remove from broiler. Top with tomato and jalapeños. Spoon sour cream in centre.

Serves 4 to 6 as snack.

SMOKED TROUT DIP

This idea came from the people at Sunbeam when they were promoting the Oskar—a terrific, compact food processor ideal for preparing foods in small amounts. This dip makes a toothsome beginning to an elegant dinner for two. Double or triple the recipe, and you've got a fabulous dip to go with drinks at a bigger gathering. Canned smoked trout is available these days in most supermarkets. It can also be found fresh or frozen.

1	egg yolk	1
2 tsp	fresh lemon juice or white wine vinegar	10 mL
2 tsp	Dijon mustard	10 mL
pinch	salt	pinch
½ cup	vegetable oil	125 mL
4 oz	skinless, boneless smoked trout	125 g
2 tsp	white wine or white wine vinegar	10 mL
2 tsp	horseradish	10 mL
¼ tsp	freshly ground pepper	1 mL

- Process egg yolk, lemon juice, mustard, salt and 1 tbsp/15 mL oil about 20 seconds in food processor or blender. Add remaining oil in thin stream until well blended. Break smoked trout in pieces and add with remaining ingredients. Process until mixture is fairly smooth. Serve with toast triangles or crackers.

Serves 2.

BLACK OLIVE DIP

Also known as tapenade in the south of France, where it is used as an appetizer spread for thin toast rounds, this also makes a lovely dip with crackers. This is an adaptation of a recipe that appeared in a 1984 article on a super cookbook called Cooking From an Italian Garden, *by Toronto couple Jon Cohen and Paola Scaravelli. Using canned olives gives milder results than the zestier Greek or Italian ones bought in bulk.*

1	dried hot red pepper or ½ tsp/2 mL hot red pepper flakes or to taste	1
1	14-oz/398-mL can pitted black olives, drained, or 6 oz/175 g Greek or Italian pitted black olives	1
1 tsp	chopped fresh oregano or ½ tsp/2 mL dried	5 mL
1 tbsp	good-quality olive oil	15 mL
1 tsp	lemon juice	5 mL
2	hard-boiled eggs, finely chopped, for garnish	2
	Lemon wedges for garnish	

• Remove seeds from hot red pepper if using; discard seeds. Place pepper, olives, oregano, olive oil and lemon juice in food processor or blender. Process until smooth, stopping to scrape down sides a few times with spatula. Spoon dip into small bowl.

• Just before serving, sprinkle hard-boiled eggs over tapenade. Garnish with lemon wedges. Serve with toasted Italian bread or crackers.

Makes about ½ cup/125 mL. Serves 4 as appetizer.

MAD KAY'S INFAMOUS CRAB DIP

Mad Kay is the affectionate nickname used by Sun *columnist Christie Blatchford for her mom. This is a family favorite when watching a game on TV. It's a terrific no-fuss recipe with loads of flavor.*

8 oz	cream cheese (room temperature)	250 g
1	7-oz/198-mL can crabmeat, well-drained	1
2 tbsp	finely chopped onion	25 mL
1 tbsp	milk	15 mL

- Preheat oven to 350°F/180°C.
- In medium bowl, beat cream cheese until soft. Add remaining ingredients. Beat until well blended. Place in ovenproof dish. Bake 20 minutes. Serve with crackers, tortilla chips or thinly sliced rye bread.

Serves 4 to 6 as appetizer.

NOTE: For more zap, add 1 tbsp/15 mL horseradish to mixture before baking. For more crunch, top with ⅓ cup/75 mL sliced almonds before baking.

HUMMUS

I remember eating hummus for the first time in the early seventies at a Lebanese restaurant in London, England. I still have a weakness for this creamy chick-pea creation. Loaded with protein and delicious when laced with lemon and garlic, hummus can be a dip or a spread. Serve it with warm triangles of pita bread.

1	19-oz/540-mL can or 2 cups/500 mL cooked chick peas (garbanzo beans)	1
¼ cup	lemon juice or to taste	50 mL
¼ cup	tahini (sesame paste)	50 mL
2	cloves garlic, minced	2
	Salt and pepper to taste	
3	pitted black olives, sliced, for garnish	3
2 tbsp	chopped fresh parsley for garnish	25 mL
	Olive oil for garnish	
	Pita bread for dipping	

- Drain chick peas, reserving liquid. Blend chick peas with ¼ cup/50 mL reserved liquid, lemon juice, tahini, garlic, salt and pepper in food processor or blender until smooth, adding more reserved liquid if necessary to obtain dipping consistency.
- To serve, spread on medium plate or place in bowl. Top with olives, sprinkle with parsley and drizzle with olive oil to thinly coat surface. Heat pita bread in oven until warm, cut in triangles and serve with hummus for dipping.

Makes about 2 cups/500 mL. Serves 8 as appetizer.

NOTE: Tahini is a sesame paste available at Greek, Middle Eastern and health food stores. For those who dislike its unusual flavor, use olive oil (or, for a low-cal version, chicken stock) instead.

BEVERLEY'S MEXICAN DIP

This dip from Beverley Lidstone took first prize in Open Kitchen's Dishiest Dip Contest in December, 1986. Lidstone is a working mother who hopes to write a cookbook for women who work and still like to cook. She suggests that hot food fans add extra hot sauce for more zap.

FIRST LAYER:

1	14-oz/398-mL can refried beans	1

- Spread beans on bottom of serving platter with raised sides.

SECOND LAYER:

1	small Haas avocado, peeled and pitted	1
2 tbsp	mayonnaise	25 mL
1 tsp	lemon juice	5 mL
1	43-g package taco seasoning mix	1
1 cup	sour cream or unflavored yogurt	250 mL

- Mash avocado with fork in bowl. Stir in mayonnaise, lemon juice, taco seasonings and sour cream. Mix well. Spread over bean layer.

THIRD LAYER:

1	large ripe fresh tomato	1
1	large green pepper, cored, seeded and finely chopped	1
6	green onions, chopped	6
½ cup	grated Cheddar or mozzarella cheese	125 mL
	Tortilla chips for dipping	

- Seed and chop tomato (see Hernando's Great Guacamole, page 10). Sprinkle tomato, green pepper, green onions and cheese over second layer. Serve with tortilla chips for dipping.

Serves 4 to 6 as appetizer.

DUNCAN'S ANTIPASTO

As with many of my favorite recipes, this is one that I gleaned from a friend. Duncan McPhee, a geologist who loves to entertain, nearly always serves this first-rate antipasto with pre-dinner drinks. Like most great dishes, it's simple to make. If you bottle the antipasto in sterilized jars, it keeps for several months in a cool, dry place. Or simply pack it in plastic containers and keep in the fridge for up to two to three weeks.

1 cup	vegetable or olive oil	250 mL
1	375-mL jar sweet pickled onions	1
½	small head cauliflower, cut in small florets	½
1	large green pepper, cored, seeded and diced	1
8 oz	button mushrooms, quartered (2 cups/500 mL)	250 g
1 cup	sliced carrots	250 mL
1 cup	sliced celery	250 mL
2 cups	dry white wine	500 mL
1 cup	cider vinegar	250 mL
4	cloves garlic, minced	4
1	bay leaf	1
1	5 ½-oz/156-mL can tomato paste	1
	Salt and pepper to taste	
2	7-oz/198-g cans chunk tuna, drained	2
½ cup	sliced dill pickles	125 mL
1	42-g jar pimientos, drained and coarsely chopped	1

• Heat oil in large heavy saucepan with lid. Add pickled onions, cauliflower, green pepper, mushrooms, carrots and celery. Bring to boil; reduce heat. Simmer, covered, 5 minutes.

• Stir in wine, vinegar, garlic and bay leaf. Bring to boil; reduce heat. Simmer, uncovered, about 10 minutes or until liquid is reduced by about one-third. Add tomato paste. Simmer 10 minutes. Add salt and pepper. Remove saucepan from heat. Remove bay leaf. Gently stir in tuna, dill pickles and pimientos.

• Return saucepan to heat. Bring mixture to boil. Vegetables should still be slightly crunchy. Remove from heat. Spoon into sterilized jars or plastic containers.

Makes about 12 cups/3 L.

ELIZABETH'S CHICKEN LIVER PÂTÉ

Elizabeth Gross, wife of Sun sports editor, George Gross, has almost as big a following when it comes to cooking as her husband does in the field of sports. This recipe appeared in my Eat Beat column in October '85 as a recommended munchie for all those Blue Jays fans who rooted for them in that crucial game against Kansas City. The Jays didn't win the World Series, but this pâté will definitely be a winner with you.

2 lb	chicken livers	1 kg
2 tbsp	butter	25 mL
½ cup	chopped onion	125 mL
½ cup	Cognac or brandy	125 mL
	Pepper to taste	
½ tsp	dried thyme	2 mL
3 tbsp	anchovy paste (room temperature)	45 mL
4 oz	cream cheese (room temperature)	125 g
½ cup	butter (room temperature)	125 mL
½ cup	chopped fresh parsley	125 mL
2	hard-boiled eggs, peeled and chopped	2

- Trim fat from chicken livers; remove bitter green sac.
- Heat 2 tbsp/25 mL butter in heavy skillet. Add livers and onion; saute over medium heat until livers lose pinkness, about 5 minutes, stirring occasionally. Cool a few minutes. Blend in food processor or blender until smooth. Do not remove from processor or blender.
- Heat Cognac in small saucepan until reduced by half. Add to liver mixture. Add pepper, thyme, anchovy paste, cream cheese and ½ cup/125 mL butter. Blend until well combined.
- Transfer to 3-cup/750-mL serving bowl or earthenware crock. Chill until firm. Garnish with parsley and chopped eggs. Serve with melba toast, crackers or thinly sliced pumpernickel bread.

Makes about 2 cups/500 mL.

RIP'N'DIP

I can't count how many people have asked for this recipe. It was originally the winner of a recipe contest at a restaurant in Toronto's Kensington Market. Serve it in a hollowed-out round pumpernickel loaf for a spectacular look, or in a dish with raw veggies or crackers for dipping.

1 cup	sour cream	250 mL
1 cup	mayonnaise	250 mL
1	10-oz/284-g package fresh spinach, cooked, squeezed dry and chopped	1
1	small red onion, finely chopped	1
1	10-oz/284-mL can water chestnuts, drained and chopped	1
1	45-g package Knorr Swiss vegetable soup mix	1
	Pepper to taste	

- Combine all ingredients in bowl. Transfer to hollowed round loaf with lid sliced off top if desired. To eat rip 'n' dip style, tear pieces off bread for dipping. Or serve with crackers or raw veggies.

Serves 8 to 10 as appetizer.

SALMON MOUSSE

A recipe from my 1985 Mother's Day eulogy to my mom's cooking, called "Mama Cooked Like This," this really simple mousse is delectably rich. It's important to use red salmon for this to give the mousse an appetizing pink color.

	Juice of ½ large lemon	
1 tsp	Worcestershire sauce	5 mL
1 tbsp	unflavored gelatin	15 mL
1	7-oz/198-mL can red salmon, drained	1
1 cup	whipping cream	250 mL
	Salt and pepper to taste	

- Lightly oil 6-cup/1.5-L mould.
- Combine lemon juice and Worcestershire in small saucepan. Sprinkle gelatin on top. Let sit a few minutes or until softened. Melt gelatin over low heat, stirring.
- Blend salmon in food processor or blender. Add gelatin mixture. Blend again. Transfer to bowl.
- Whip cream in separate bowl until soft peaks form. Fold into salmon mixture. Add salt and pepper. Spoon into prepared mould. Chill until set, about 2 hours. Unmould and serve with crackers, toast triangles or melba toast.

Serves 6 to 8.

CHEESY POTATO SKINS

These are one of the most popular snacks around and can be a light supper, an accompaniment to drinks at a party, or just what the doctor ordered when the hungries hit.

4	large baking potatoes, unpeeled	4
2 tbsp	vegetable or olive oil	25 mL
2 tbsp	Dijon mustard	25 mL
1 cup	grated cheese (Swiss, Cheddar, Monterey Jack, etc.)	250 mL
4	green onions, chopped	4
4	slices crisp cooked bacon, crumbled	4

• Preheat oven to 400°F/200°C.

• Scrub potatoes; prick with fork. Bake 1 hour or until tender. Cut in half lengthwise. Scoop out flesh with spoon, leaving about ½ inch/1 cm clinging to skin. (Save scooped out potato for mashed potatoes, pancakes, etc.) Cut each half lengthwise again.

• Brush potato quarters all over with oil. Brush with mustard. Place on ungreased cookie sheet.

• Bake about 20 minutes or until crisp and golden brown.

• Combine cheese, green onions and crumbled bacon in small bowl. Sprinkle over potato quarters. Return to oven or place under broiler. Cook a few minutes or until cheese melts. Serve with sour cream, blue cheese dip and/or taco sauce.

Serves 4.

SESAME CHICKEN FINGERS

This variation on the chicken finger theme makes a good one-bite party snack and was recommended in "Ice 'n' Easy Appetizers," an article I wrote on Christmas party hors d'oeuvres. These have the great advantage of being easy to freeze. Cook, freeze and then reheat in the oven at party time.

MARINADE:

1 tbsp	wine vinegar	15 mL
2 tbsp	soy sauce	25 mL
2 tbsp	honey	25 mL
2 tbsp	dry sherry	25 mL
1 tsp	chopped fresh ginger root	5 mL
1	clove garlic, minced	1
2 tbsp	vegetable oil	25 mL

- Combine marinade ingredients in shallow dish. Mix well.

| 6 | single chicken breasts, skin and bones removed | 6 |
| ⅓ cup | sesame seeds | 75 mL |

- Slice chicken breasts lengthwise into strips 1 inch/2 cm wide. Place in dish with marinade; toss to coat. Let marinate, covered, in fridge for 6 hours or overnight, turning occasionally.
- Preheat oven to 400°F/200°C. Place sesame seeds in shallow dish.
- Remove chicken from marinade and roll in sesame seeds, coating well. Place on lightly greased baking sheet. Bake 10 to 15 minutes or until cooked. Serve with chutney, Chinese plum sauce or favorite dip.

Makes about 24.

CHEESE DREAMS

These are tasty and easy to make. I suggested them in an article on cocktail appetizers for Christmas. But they're good on almost any occasion when finger food is on the menu. The party nibbly of all time, this version comes from one of Toronto's top caterers, Allison Cumming.

12	slices white bread	12
½ cup	melted butter	125 mL
⅓ cup	slivered almonds	75 mL
2 cups	grated Cheddar cheese (8 oz/250 g)	500 mL
4	slices bacon, cooked and chopped	4
2	egg yolks, lightly beaten	2
1 tbsp	Dijon mustard	15 mL
1 tbsp	mayonnaise	15 mL
	Salt and pepper to taste	

- Preheat oven to 350°F/180°C.
- Trim crusts from bread. Cut each slice into four triangles. Brush one side of each slice with melted butter. Press each triangle, butter side up, into muffin tins (mini ones work best but regular size will do).
- Bake 4 to 5 minutes or until toasted.
- Shaking constantly, toast almonds in heavy skillet over low heat until golden brown, about 5 minutes.
- Combine cheese, bacon, egg yolks, mustard, mayonnaise, salt, pepper and toasted almonds in bowl. Mix well. Spoon into toasted bread cases. Return to oven 3 to 5 minutes or until heated through and golden brown. Serve warm.

Makes about 4 dozen.

SPINACH FETA PHYLLO TRIANGLES

The Greek word for these marvellous munchies is spanakopita. They have understandably become a North American party favorite. Phyllo pastry, thank goodness, is now available frozen at most supermarkets. The busy host/ess will be happy to hear that these triangles can be frozen (this must be done before they are cooked), then baked at the last minute.

1 tbsp	olive oil	15 mL
1	small onion, finely chopped	1
1	10-oz/284-g package fresh spinach, cooked, squeezed dry and chopped	1
	Freshly grated nutmeg to taste	
1 tsp	dried or 2 tbsp/25 mL chopped fresh dill	5 mL
⅓ cup	ricotta cheese	75 mL
¼ cup	crumbled feta cheese	50 mL
	Salt and pepper to taste	
10	sheets frozen phyllo dough, thawed	10
½ cup	melted butter	125 mL

• Heat oil in heavy skillet. Add onion; saute until soft, about 5 minutes. Add spinach; cook over low heat until dry. Stir in nutmeg. Transfer mixture to bowl. Cool. Stir in dill, cheeses, salt and pepper. Mix to combine.

• Preheat oven to 350°F/180°C.

• Remove one sheet of phyllo from package. Cover remaining sheets with barely dampened tea towel. Brush sheet with melted butter, working quickly so dough doesn't dry out. Cut in strips 3 inches/6 cm wide. Place 1 tsp/5 mL filling in bottom corner of each strip. Fold dough over filling to form triangle; repeat until you reach top of strip and have one triangle. Brush with more melted butter. Repeat with remaining dough until filling is used up.

• Bake 15 to 20 minutes until golden brown.

Makes about 4 dozen.

FETTUCCINE ZUCCHINI

Mark McEwan, chef and co-owner of Toronto's Pronto Ristorante, created this incredible appetizer using narrow zucchini strips instead of noodles. The creamy sauce is laced with goat's cheese and sun-dried tomatoes. What a heavenly combination!

4	medium unpeeled zucchini	4
1	small ripe fresh tomato	1
1 tbsp	butter	15 mL
2 tsp	chopped shallots or onions	10 mL
2	cloves garlic, finely chopped	2
	Salt and pepper to taste	
pinch	freshly grated nutmeg	pinch
¼ cup	dry white wine	50 mL
1 cup	whipping cream	250 mL
2 tbsp	sun-dried tomatoes, cut in julienne strips	25 mL
2 tsp	chopped fresh thyme or 1 tsp/5mL dried	10 mL
¼ cup	crumbled goat's cheese (2 oz/60 g)	50 mL

• Cut zucchini in half lengthwise. Scoop out seeds with spoon or melon-baller. Cut each half in long, narrow strips to resemble fettuccine noodles.

• Cut tomato in half horizontally. To remove seeds, squeeze each half gently. Chop tomato coarsely.

• Bring pot of salted water to boil.

• Heat butter in large heavy skillet. Add shallots; saute until softened, about 3 minutes. Add garlic, salt, pepper and nutmeg. Saute about 1 minute. Add wine, stirring to scrape up bits from bottom of pan. Add cream. Bring to boil; continue boiling until sauce thickens slightly, about 1 minute. Add chopped tomato, sun-dried tomatoes, thyme and goat's cheese. Whisk until sauce is smooth.

• Blanch zucchini by plunging into pot of boiling water for 10 seconds. Drain. Add to sauce. Toss to coat.

Serves 4 to 6 as appetizer or side dish with meat, poultry or fish.

GINGERY PARSNIP SOUP

For some reason, the parsnip has an undeservedly bad reputation. There are few things as yummy as peeled and halved parsnips roasted in the same pan as your festive bird or roast of beef. Cooked into a soup and laced with ginger, parsnips have a creamy texture and a zesty yet delicate taste. Eaten with some crusty wholewheat bread and a hunk of cheese, this makes a budget meal to remember.

3 tbsp	butter	45 mL
1	medium onion, chopped	1
1 lb	parsnips, peeled and chopped (about 3)	500 g
1	medium potato, peeled and chopped	1
5 cups	chicken stock	1.25 L
1 tsp	chopped peeled fresh ginger root	5 mL
	Salt and pepper to taste	
¾ cup	whipping or light cream or milk	175 mL

• Melt butter in large saucepan. Add onion; saute until soft, about 5 minutes. Add parsnips, potato, chicken stock and ginger root. Bring to boil; reduce heat. Simmer 25 minutes or until vegetables are tender. Blend in batches in food processor or blender until smooth. Return to saucepan. Add salt, pepper and cream or milk. Cook until heated through.

Serves 4 to 6.

GREEN BEAN SOUP

I once made soup with green beans purely by accident, since they were plentiful in the market that day. What a pleasant surprise! This flavorful vegetable makes one of the smoothest, tastiest soups I know. This version comes from Le Soufflé restaurant in Toronto. You can omit the leeks if desired and add another cup/250 mL of green beans instead.

1 lb	green beans, topped and tailed	500 g
4 cups	chicken stock	1 L
2	leeks (white and light green parts only)	2
2 tbsp	butter	25 mL
2 tbsp	all-purpose flour	25 mL
¾ cup	whipping or light cream	175 mL
	Salt and pepper to taste	

• Cut beans in 1-inch/2-cm pieces, reserving a few whole beans for garnish. Place in large saucepan. Add chicken stock. Bring to boil; reduce heat. Simmer.

- Meanwhile, slice leeks in half lengthwise; clean well to remove grit. Cut each half into 1-inch/2-cm pieces.
- Melt butter in heavy skillet. Add leeks; saute until soft, about 5 minutes. Sprinkle flour over leeks, stirring constantly. Cook about 1 minute, stirring.
- Add leek mixture to bean mixture. Whisking constantly, bring to boil. Reduce heat; simmer 30 minutes or until vegetables are soft. Blend, in batches if necessary, in food processor or blender until smooth. Return to saucepan. Add cream, salt and pepper. Cook until heated through.
- Cut reserved beans into very thin julienne strips. Add to hot soup for garnish.

Serves 6.

CREAMY AVOCADO SOUP

The avocado is a quirky fruit that masquerades as a vegetable and combines a sky-high calorie count with loads of vitamins and minerals. This soup gives new meaning to the words "silky smooth" and is wonderful eaten cold on a steamy summer's day along with salad and a French baguette.

2	large ripe avocados, peeled, pitted and diced	2
1 cup	light cream	250 mL
4 cups	chicken or vegetable stock	1 L
2 tbsp	dry sherry	25 mL
2 tbsp	lemon juice	25 mL
	Salt and pepper to taste	
	Crushed tortilla chips for garnish (optional)	

- Reserve about ½ cup/125 mL avocado for garnish. Place remaining avocado and cream in food processor or blender. Blend until smooth.
- Bring stock to boil in saucepan. Reduce heat to simmer. Whisk in avocado puree. Add sherry, lemon juice, salt and pepper. Cook, stirring, until heated through. Serve warm or chilled. Garnish with reserved avocado and crushed tortilla chips if using.

Serves 6.

BLACK BEAN SOUP

Another recipe from a low-fat menu devised by student chefs at the Stratford Chefs' School in Stratford, Ontario. This fabulous soup, which hails from South America, is also high in fibre and brimming with flavor. Garnished with a dollop of mock sour cream (low-cal crème fraîche), it looks as wonderful as it tastes. Black beans, also known as turtle beans, can be found in bulk food stores and stores specializing in Mexican and/or South American ingredients.

1½ cups	dried black (turtle) beans	375 mL
3 cups	water	750 mL
6 cups	chicken, beef or vegetable stock	1.5 L
3 tbsp	corn, safflower or sunflower oil	45 mL
1	medium onion, chopped	1
3	cloves garlic, finely chopped	3
1	stalk celery, finely chopped	1
1	carrot, peeled and finely chopped	1
1 tsp	dried oregano, thyme or mixed herbs	5 mL
pinch	cayenne pepper	pinch
¼ cup	dry sherry	50 mL
	Juice of 1 lemon	
	Salt and pepper to taste	
	Mock sour cream for garnish	
	(recipe below)	
¼ cup	Mexican salsa for garnish (optional)	50 mL
2 tbsp	chopped fresh parsley for garnish (optional)	25 mL

• Soak beans in water 6 hours or overnight. Drain; discard soaking liquid. Transfer beans to large saucepan with lid. Add chicken stock. Bring to boil; reduce heat. Simmer, partially covered, about 1½ hours or until beans are almost tender.

• Heat oil in heavy skillet. Add onion, garlic, celery and carrot; saute until onion is softened, about 5 minutes. Add mixture to beans along with oregano and cayenne. Bring to boil; reduce heat. Simmer, covered, until beans are tender, about 1 hour. Puree all or half of mixture in food processor or blender, in batches if necessary, until smooth. Return to saucepan. Stir in sherry, lemon juice, salt and pepper. Cook until heated through.

• Pour into bowls and swirl a spoonful of mock sour cream (recipe below) into each serving. Top with a little Mexican salsa and/or a little chopped fresh parsley if desired.

Serves 6 to 8.

MOCK SOUR CREAM:

1 cup	low-fat cottage cheese	250 mL
2 tbsp	skim milk	25 mL
1 tbsp	lemon juice	15 mL
pinch	salt	pinch

• Blend all ingredients in food processor or blender until smooth.

Makes about 1 cup/250 mL.

RED PEPPER SOUP

I can hardly get enough of sweet red peppers when they're in season in the fall. This soup is slightly sweet, silky smooth and pretty as a picture. Use milk instead of cream if you're counting calories.

2 tbsp	vegetable oil or butter	25 mL
1	small onion, chopped	1
4	sweet red peppers, cored, seeded and sliced	4
1	medium potato, peeled and chopped	1
3 cups	chicken stock	750 mL
½ cup	whipping or light cream	125 mL
2 tbsp	lemon juice	25 mL
	Salt and pepper to taste	
2 tbsp	chopped fresh dill or parsley for garnish	25 mL

• Heat oil in large saucepan with lid. Add onion and red peppers; saute until softened, about 10 minutes. Add potato and chicken stock. Bring to boil; reduce heat. Simmer, covered, about 30 minutes or until potatoes are cooked. Transfer to food processor or blender. Blend, in batches if necessary, until smooth.

• Return to saucepan. Add cream, lemon juice, salt and pepper. Cook until heated through. Serve hot or cold garnished with chopped dill or parsley.

Serves 4.

BALKAN BEET SOUP

A super, low-fat cold borscht from Anne Lindsay's terrific book, Smart Cooking. *Loaded with calcium, phosphorus and vitamin C.*

¼ cup	sour cream	50 mL
¼ cup	low-fat cottage cheese	50 mL
2 cups	buttermilk	500 mL
2	medium beets, cooked, peeled and cubed	2
1	hard-boiled egg, peeled and chopped	1
¼	English cucumber, unpeeled and diced	¼
¼ cup	chopped fresh parsley	50 mL
3 tbsp	sliced radishes	45 mL
2 tbsp	chopped fresh chives or green onions	25 mL
	Salt and pepper to taste	

• Blend sour cream and cottage cheese in food processor or blender until smooth. Blend in buttermilk. Transfer to bowl. Refrigerate.
• Just before serving, divide beets among four bowls.
• Stir remaining ingredients into buttermilk mixture. Pour over beets.

Serves 4.

BRIDGESIDE CLAM CHOWDER

An ever-popular standby, this version of clam chowder comes from By the Bridge, an excellent seafood restaurant in Toronto.

2 tbsp	butter	25 mL
2 tbsp	chopped celery	25 mL
1	medium onion, chopped	1
2 tbsp	all-purpose flour	25 mL
1	5-oz/142-g can baby clams, drained (reserve liquid)	1
2	medium potatoes, peeled and diced	2
¼ tsp	celery salt	1 mL
	Salt and white pepper to taste	
2 cups	milk	500 mL
1 cup	whipping cream	250 mL
	Chopped fresh parsley for garnish	

• Melt butter in large heavy saucepan with lid. Add celery and onion; saute until softened, about 5 minutes. Sprinkle on flour; stir until blended. Slowly stir in reserved clam liquid. Add potatoes, celery salt, salt and white pepper. Bring to boil; reduce heat. Simmer, covered, 10 minutes. Add clams, milk and cream. Bring to boil; reduce heat. Simmer 15 minutes. Garnish with chopped parsley.

Serves 4.

CURRIED BUTTERNUT SQUASH SOUP

In the winter of '86, I visited the Stratford Chefs' School—a unique idea whereby several of the town's top restaurants band together to hone local chefs in their art during the theatre off-season. The school had a low-fat dinner on the menu, and a tasty meal it was, too. This was one of the soups; it is a great way to use almost any of the beautiful squash that are so plentiful in fall and winter.

2 tbsp	vegetable oil	25 mL
1	medium onion, finely chopped	1
2 tsp	curry powder or to taste	10 mL
1	butternut squash (about 3 lb/1.5 kg), peeled, seeded and chopped	1
2	apples, peeled, cored and chopped	2
3 cups	chicken stock	750 mL
1 cup	unsweetened apple juice	250 mL
	Salt and pepper to taste	
	Rind of 1 lime or lemon, finely slivered, for garnish	

• Heat oil in large heavy saucepan with lid. Add onion and curry powder. Cook over low heat, covered, stirring occasionally, until onion is soft, about 5 minutes. Add squash, apples and chicken stock. Bring to boil; reduce heat. Simmer, partially covered, until squash and apples are tender, about 25 minutes. Transfer squash mixture to food processor or blender with slotted spoon. Add 1 cup/250 mL cooking liquid. Blend until smooth.
• Return blended mixture to liquid in saucepan. Add apple juice, salt and pepper. Cook until heated through. Garnish with lime or lemon rind.

Serves 6.

NOTE: If you like a thicker, richer soup, add ½ cup/125 mL whipping cream to soup at end of cooking and heat through.

PUMPKIN SOUP

It has always seemed like a terrible waste to me to throw away that Hallowe'en pumpkin, with its eminently edible flesh. Even if you go out and buy one of those golden gourds just for this soup, you won't be disappointed. Omit the wine if you like and use milk instead of cream if you're counting calories. This recipe makes a lot of soup, since it uses the flesh of a medium-large pumpkin. Any leftovers freeze well (without the cream).

3 tbsp	vegetable oil	45 mL
1	small onion, chopped	1
6 cups	diced pumpkin flesh (about 3 lb/1.5 kg)	1.5 L
1	medium potato, peeled and diced	1
6 cups	chicken or beef stock	1.5 L
½ cup	Marsala or other sweet dessert wine	125 mL
1 tsp	dried thyme	5 mL
	Salt and pepper to taste	
½ cup	whipping or light cream or milk	125 mL
	Toasted pumpkin seeds for garnish	
	(see note)	

• Heat oil in large heavy saucepan with lid. Add onion; saute until softened, about 5 minutes. Add pumpkin. Saute 15 minutes, stirring occasionally. Add potato and stock. Bring to boil; reduce heat. Simmer, covered, 30 minutes or until pumpkin is tender. Add Marsala and thyme. Transfer to food processor or blender. Blend, in batches if necessary, until smooth.

• Return to saucepan. Add salt, pepper and cream or milk. Cook until heated through. Serve garnished with toasted pumpkin seeds.

Serves 8 to 10.

NOTE: To toast pumpkin seeds, rinse to remove strings and pulp and pat dry with paper towels. Toss in bowl with enough vegetable oil to coat lightly. Sprinkle lightly with salt. Spread on cookie sheet in one layer. Toast in 350°F/ 180°C oven 20 minutes or until golden, stirring at intervals. Makes a terrific snack.

VEGETABLES AND SALADS

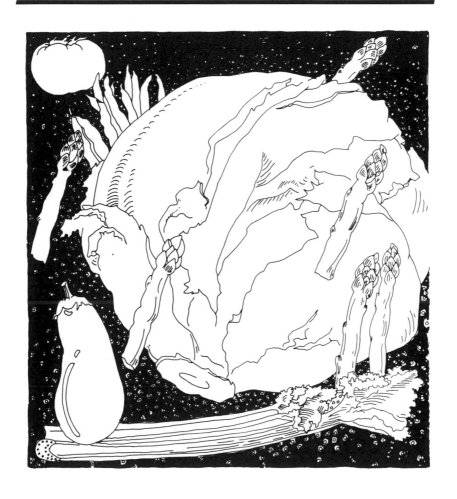

RED CABBAGE WITH YOGURT AND ALMONDS

My vegetarian friend, Polly Evans, is one of the best cooks I know. This is one of her recipes, which I used in an article called "What's Cooking" to illustrate a point of food science when writing about the mammoth Food Show at the Ontario Science Centre in 1986. The acid of the yogurt (you can also use sour cream) helps the red cabbage retain its gorgeous color. This dish goes well with roast meat, chicken and especially duck or goose.

½ cup	slivered almonds	125 mL
¼ cup	butter	50 mL
1 tbsp	paprika	15 mL
	Salt and pepper to taste	
1	small head red cabbage, coarsely shredded	1
	(6 to 8 cups/1.5 to 2 L)	
½ cup	unflavored yogurt or sour cream	125 mL

- Preheat oven to 350°F/180°C.
- Shaking constantly, toast almonds in heavy skillet over low heat until golden brown, about 5 minutes.
- Melt butter in large heavy casserole. Stir in paprika, salt and pepper. Add cabbage. Saute, stirring, 5 minutes. Stir in yogurt. Sprinkle on almonds.
- Bake, uncovered, 30 minutes or until cabbage is tender-crisp.

Serves 4 to 6.

BARBECUED CORN

What would a barbecue be without corn? This nifty method uses the corn's own husk as a cooking utensil.

4	cobs corn	4
4 tbsp	butter	50 mL
	Salt and pepper to taste	

- Peel corn husks back, leaving them attached at stalk end. Spread each cob with butter. Sprinkle with salt and pepper. Pull husks back over cobs. Secure with string. Soak in cold water 15 minutes so string won't burn.
- Grill cobs over medium coals about 15 minutes, turning at intervals. To serve, remove string and husks.

Serves 4.

SWEET POTATO PUREE

From Pierre Dubrulle, who operates his own cooking school for chefs in Vancouver. A great sidekick to turkey at Thanksgiving or Christmas.

6	sweet potatoes, unpeeled	6
1 tsp	powdered ginger	5 mL
3 tbsp	dark rum	45 mL
2 tbsp	butter	25 mL
1 cup	chopped hazelnuts (filberts)	250 mL
¾ cup	milk, heated	175 mL

- Preheat oven to 350°F/180°C.
- Place potatoes on ungreased cookie sheet. Bake 1 hour or until tender. Cool. Cut each potato in half. Scoop out flesh with spoon. Press flesh through fine sieve or puree in food mill. Place in saucepan.
- Combine ginger and rum in separate small saucepan. Bring to boil, stirring. Add to potatoes with butter, hazelnuts and milk. Mix well and cook until heated through.

Serves 4 to 6.

TURNIP PEAR PUREE

A wonderful way to cook that much underrated vegetable—turnip, also known as rutabaga. Pureeing gives it a creamy texture that will have even the kids asking for seconds. If the pears are not soft, add them to the turnip halfway through the cooking.

1	medium turnip (rutabaga), peeled and cubed	1
2	very ripe pears, peeled, cored and cubed	2
3 tbsp	sour cream or unflavored yogurt	45 mL
1 tbsp	butter	15 mL
	Salt and pepper to taste	
pinch	freshly grated nutmeg	pinch

- Cook turnip in boiling salted water until tender, about 20 minutes. Drain well. Puree together with pears in food processor or blender, in batches if necessary. Return mixture to saucepan. Add remaining ingredients. Cook a few minutes over medium-low heat or until heated through.

Serves 4 to 6.

CELERY ROOT APPLE PUREE

As silken smooth as the best mashed potatoes, celery root makes a terrific vegetable puree.
My teenaged daughter loves this dish. So will you. Celery root, also known as celeriac, is
plentiful in fall and early winter and is also delicious shredded raw in salads.

It is important to use Delicious apples in this recipe; a tarter apple such as Granny
Smith could cause the milk to curdle.

1	medium celery root (about 1 lb/500 g), washed, peeled and diced	1
2 cups	milk	500 mL
2	Delicious apples, cored, peeled and diced	2
	Salt and pepper to taste	

• Place celery root in large saucepan with lid. Pour on milk, adding a little more if needed to just cover celery root. Bring to boil; reduce heat. Simmer, covered, 10 minutes. Add apples. Simmer 10 minutes more or until celery root is tender. Drain, reserving cooking liquid.

• Puree celery root mixture in food processor or blender, in batches if necessary, adding enough cooking liquid to give consistency of mashed potatoes. Add salt and pepper.

Serves 4 to 6.

NOTE: If making ahead, reheat puree over low heat in saucepan or bake in covered casserole in 300°F/150°C oven about 30 minutes or until heated through.

PEPERONATA

My mother used to cook this in the fall, when sweet peppers were at their peak. It should be
made with plenty of garlic and is beautiful prepared with a mixture of red, orange and yellow
peppers. A super lunch dish when served with cold meat or cheese, or the perfect side dish to
roasted or barbecued meat, chicken or fish.

6	sweet peppers in assorted colors, cored and seeded	6
¼ cup	olive oil	50 mL
1	medium onion, sliced	1
3	cloves garlic, finely chopped	3
2 to 3	ripe fresh tomatoes, seeded and chopped	2 to 3
¼ cup	chopped fresh basil or 1 tbsp/15 mL dried	50 mL
	Salt and freshly ground black pepper to taste	

- Cut peppers lengthwise in strips ¼ inch/5 mm wide.
- Heat oil in large heavy saucepan with lid. Add onion and garlic. Saute, uncovered, until softened, about 5 minutes. Do not brown. Add tomatoes, basil, salt and pepper. Cook, uncovered, over low heat, about 10 minutes. Stir in sliced peppers. Cook, covered, 10 minutes more or until peppers are tender.

Serves 6 to 8 as side dish.

RED PEPPER SAUCE

Once I learned how to roast peppers, there was no turning back. Cooking them this way enhances their flavor and results in a succulent, juicy texture. I use this sauce on all kinds of barbecued meat, especially chicken, as well as on fish and pasta.

2 tbsp	olive or vegetable oil	25 mL
2	large sweet red peppers, cored, seeded and chopped	2
1	small onion, chopped	1
1	clove garlic, finely chopped	1
¼ cup	dry white wine	50 mL
1 tsp	chopped fresh basil or ½ tsp/2 mL dried	5 mL
	Salt and pepper to taste	
2 tbsp	whipping cream (optional)	25 mL

- Heat oil in heavy skillet or saucepan. Add peppers, onion and garlic. Saute until soft, about 5 minutes. Add wine. Bring mixture to boil; reduce heat. Simmer, uncovered, about 10 minutes.
- Puree mixture in food processor or blender until smooth. Return sauce to saucepan. Stir in basil, salt, pepper and cream if using. Cook until heated through.

Serves 4 to 6 as sauce to accompany meat, poultry, fish or pasta.

NOTE: For even better flavor, roast peppers (page 34), then peel, core and seed them over a bowl to catch juices. Puree peppers with juices and remaining ingredients as in above recipe. If sauce is too thick, add a little more wine or cream. If too thin, simmer until thickened.

STEWED RED PEPPERS

Another luscious idea for using all those sweet peppers in the fall. Stewing them this way in brown sugar and butter caramelizes the peppers slightly, with delicious results.

3	sweet red peppers, cored and seeded	3
3 tbsp	brown sugar	45 mL
3 tbsp	butter	45 mL
½ cup	dry white wine	125 mL
3 tbsp	balsamic, sherry or cider vinegar	45 mL
	Salt and pepper to taste	

• Slice peppers lengthwise into strips ¼ inch/5 mm wide. Combine with brown sugar and butter in heavy skillet or saucepan with lid. Cook, covered, over low heat, 45 minutes, stirring occasionally. Be careful not to burn. Add wine and vinegar. Bring to boil; reduce heat. Simmer, uncovered, stirring occasionally, 15 minutes or until thick. Add salt and pepper.

Serves 4.

ROASTED PEPPERS

A barbecue favorite that's a must in early fall when peppers of every hue are brimming out of bushel baskets at all the vegetable markets. You can freeze the roasted and peeled peppers or store them in good-quality olive oil.

Sweet peppers (red, green or yellow)
Cloves garlic, peeled and sliced
Salt and pepper
Olive oil

• Preheat broiler or barbecue grill.
• Place peppers under broiler or over medium-high barbecue grill. Cook, turning at intervals, until skin is thoroughly blistered and charred, about 10 minutes.
• Place each pepper in a brown paper bag. Twist top to seal. Let sit about 10 minutes. Remove from bag. Peel off skin with small sharp knife. Core, seed and slice.
• To store roasted peppers, arrange slices in layers in bowl. Place garlic slices between each layer. Sprinkle each layer with salt, pepper and olive oil. Cover and store in fridge. Serve at room temperature as appetizer or accompaniment to meat, poultry or fish.

SUN'S TEX-MEX STUFFED SPUDS

This recipe was created especially for Sun *readers by Judy Wells, co-author of* The Noble Spud, *as part of a 1986 St. Patrick's Day eulogy to that most wonderful of veg.*

6	large baking potatoes	6
1 tbsp	vegetable oil	15 mL
1	medium onion, finely chopped	1
1	clove garlic, finely chopped	1
8 oz	ground beef	250 g
1	14-oz/398-mL can refried beans	1
1	8-oz/227-mL jar mild, medium or spicy Mexican salsa (about 1 cup/250 mL)	1
	Salt and pepper to taste	
1 cup	sour cream or unflavored yogurt	250 mL
2 tbsp	finely chopped green pepper	25 mL
2 tbsp	finely chopped fresh parsley	25 mL
	Corn chips for garnish	

- Preheat oven to 400°F/200°C.
- Scrub potatoes; prick with fork. Place on baking sheet. Bake 1 hour or until tender.
- Heat oil in large skillet. Add onion; saute until soft, about 5 minutes. Add garlic and ground beef. Saute, stirring, until beef is browned. Drain off fat. Add refried beans and Mexican salsa. Add salt and pepper. Simmer, stirring occasionally, 40 to 50 minutes or until thickened.
- Cut an "X" in top of each potato. Squeeze to loosen flesh. Fill potatoes with beef mixture. Top with sour cream, green pepper and parsley. Serve with corn chips on side.

Serves 6 as main course.

Summery Baked Potatoes

This recipe was also part of a St. Pat's day tribute to the spud. Stuffed baked potatoes make a nutritious, tasty meal that's quick to prepare and sure to be a hit with the whole family. And don't forget to eat the skin—it's loaded with fibre, not to mention great flavor.

4	large baking potatoes	4
1	small red onion, finely chopped	1
1	small green pepper, cored, seeded and finely chopped	1
1 cup	grated Cheddar cheese	250 mL
	Salt and pepper to taste	
2 tbsp	chopped fresh parsley	25 mL
1 tbsp	butter (room temperature)	15 mL
2 tbsp	chopped green onion or fresh chives	25 mL
2 tsp	lemon juice	10 mL
1	egg, beaten	1

• Preheat oven to 400°F/200°C.
• Scrub potatoes; prick with fork. Place on baking sheet. Bake 1 hour or until tender.
• Reduce oven temperature to 350°F/180°C.
• Combine red onion, green pepper, cheese, salt, pepper, parsley, butter and green onion in bowl.
• Cut thick lid off each potato, reserving lid. Scoop out flesh, leaving some attached to skin for support. Add scooped-out flesh to vegetable/cheese mixture. Mix in lemon juice and egg. Spoon mixture into potato shells. Replace lids. Place on baking sheet. Bake 15 minutes or until heated through.

Serves 4.

Prize Potato Salad

This recipe from Edweena Duguay was the winner in Open Kitchen's Prize Potato Salad Contest. Japanese rice vinegar is the key ingredient; it adds a unique and pleasant taste, but wine, tarragon or cider vinegar will do in a pinch.

8	new potatoes, scrubbed	8
4	hard-boiled eggs, peeled	4
1	medium red onion, peeled	1
1 cup	cooked peas (frozen, thawed or fresh)	250 mL
¾ cup	Miracle Whip salad dressing	175 mL
⅓ cup	Japanese rice vinegar	75 mL

Salt and pepper to taste
Paprika and chopped fresh parsley for garnish

• Cook potatoes in salted water until tender. Peel if desired. Cut into bite-sized pieces. Place in large bowl.
• Cut 3 eggs into ¼-inch/5-mm slices, then in half. Add to bowl. Cut onion into ¼-inch/5-mm slices, then in quarters. Add to bowl along with peas. Toss.
• Combine Miracle Whip, vinegar, salt and pepper in small bowl. Add dressing to potato mixture. Toss. Slice remaining egg. Arrange on top of salad. Sprinkle with paprika and parsley.

Serves 4 to 6.

STELLE'S POLENTA

Inspired chef Greg Couillard, co-owner of Stelle restaurant in Toronto, makes the best polenta I've ever tasted. Follow this recipe, then layer the cooked polenta with grated cheese, some ricotta laced with nutmeg, and cooked spinach. Bake it in the oven and serve with homemade tomato sauce, and you've got a meatless meal to remember. Use fine cornmeal; the coarse stuff does not give the same results.

4 cups	water	1 L
1 tsp	salt	5 mL
1 cup	fine yellow cornmeal	250 mL
½ cup	corn, frozen and thawed or canned and drained	125 mL
¼ cup	freshly grated Romano or Parmesan cheese	50 mL
¼ cup	chopped fresh basil	50 mL
2 tbsp	butter	25 mL

• Bring water and salt to boil in heavy saucepan. Gradually add cornmeal, pouring through wire whisk and whisking constantly. When mixture starts to thicken, reduce heat to low. Cook 20 to 30 minutes, stirring frequently, until mixture resembles cooked pudding or cream of wheat. Stir in corn, cheese, basil and butter. Serve at once or pack into unbuttered 8-cup/2-L ovenproof dish.
• To reheat, bake, covered, in 375°F/190°C oven 15 to 20 minutes. Serve as side dish with stewed meat or homemade tomato sauce and freshly grated Parmesan on the side. You can also cut polenta in slices, brush it with oil and grill under broiler or on barbecue as a sidekick to barbecued ribs, chicken, etc.

Serves 6 to 8.

SAFFRON RICE

This is a must when making an East Indian meal. If you can't find saffron (beware of imitations), substitute a teaspoon of ground turmeric. I highly recommend the delicate, thin-grained Basmati rice, available at any East Indian grocery store.

¼ cup	slivered or sliced almonds	50 mL
1 tsp	saffron threads	5 mL
2 cups	Basmati or other long-grain rice	500 mL
2 tbsp	vegetable oil	25 mL
½	cinnamon stick	½
2	whole cloves	2
1	small onion, chopped	1
4 cups	boiling water	1 L
1 tsp	salt	5 mL
	Seeds of 3 cardamom pods or ½ tsp/2 mL cardamom seeds (optional)	
¼ cup	raisins	50 mL

• Shaking constantly, toast almonds in heavy skillet over low heat for a few minutes or until golden.

• Place saffron threads in small bowl. Pour on 3 tbsp/45 mL boiling water. Let sit 10 minutes.

• To wash rice, place in bowl and cover with cold water. Rub grains lightly between fingers until water runs clear and all surface starch has been removed. Drain well.

• Heat oil over medium heat in heavy saucepan with lid. Add cinnamon stick, cloves and onion. Saute until onion is soft, about 5 minutes. Add rice. Saute 5 minutes or until rice is golden. Add boiling water, salt and cardamom seeds. Bring to boil, stirring. Stir in saffron and its soaking liquid. Reduce heat; simmer, covered, 15 minutes. Stir in raisins. Simmer, covered, 10 minutes more or until rice is tender and all liquid is absorbed. Fluff with fork. Top with toasted almonds. Remove cinnamon stick and cloves.

Serves 6 to 8 as side dish with curry, tandoori chicken, etc.

TABBOULEH

What a delectable way to get all the fibre, vitamins and minerals of that nutty grain called bulgur—without even cooking it! This is a Middle Eastern dish that makes a great accompaniment to barbecued meat, especially lamb or chicken. Don't stint on the parsley—it's an essential ingredient that's loaded with flavor as well as nutrients.

1 cup	fine or medium bulgur	250 mL
1½ cups	chopped fresh parsley	375 mL
⅓ cup	chopped fresh mint	75 mL
½ cup	chopped green or sweet red pepper	125 mL
½ cup	chopped green onion	125 mL
	Juice of 1 lemon	
½ cup	olive oil	125 mL
1	clove garlic, minced	1
1 tbsp	chopped fresh basil or ½ tsp/2 mL dried	15 mL
	Salt and freshly ground black pepper to taste	

- Place bulgur in bowl. Add boiling water, just enough to cover. Let sit until bulgur is softened, about 1 hour. Drain well.
- Transfer drained bulgur to serving bowl. Stir in parsley, mint, green or red pepper and green onion.
- In small bowl, whisk together lemon juice, olive oil, garlic, basil, salt and pepper until well blended. Pour over bulgur mixture. Stir to combine.

Serves 4 to 6.

CREAMY CUCUMBER DRESSING

A refreshing summery salad dressing from Foodland Ontario; it's great on almost any salad.

1 cup	mayonnaise	250 mL
½ cup	sour cream or unflavored yogurt	125 mL
1 cup	peeled, sliced cucumber	250 mL
1 tbsp	chopped fresh dill	15 mL
1 tsp	lemon juice	5 mL
1 tsp	granulated sugar	5 mL
½ tsp	horseradish (optional)	2 mL
	Salt and pepper to taste	
pinch	cayenne pepper (optional)	pinch

- Process all ingredients in food processor or blender until smooth.

Makes about 2 cups/500 mL.

SUPER CAESAR DRESSING

By now I assume that you know how to toss together toasted croutons, torn Romaine lettuce and a sprinkling of freshly grated Parmesan to come up with a Caesar salad. But there is always room for an improved Caesar dressing. This one comes from Claire Stancer's new salad dressing cookbook, and makes enough for two heads of Romaine lettuce. Any leftover dressing will keep at least a week in the fridge, stored in an airtight container.

3	cloves garlic, minced	3
4	anchovy fillets	4
1 tsp	granulated sugar	5 mL
1 tsp	Dijon mustard	5 mL
2 tbsp	chopped fresh parsley	25 mL
½ tsp	Worcestershire sauce	2 mL
3 tbsp	wine vinegar	45 mL
1	egg	1
¼ tsp	ground black pepper	1 mL
3 tbsp	freshly grated Parmesan cheese	45 mL
¾ cup	olive or vegetable oil	175 mL

• Blend all ingredients except oil in food processor or blender until smooth. With machine running, add oil in thin stream. (Don't overprocess or dressing will get too thick.)

Makes about 1 cup/250 mL.

TOFU MAYONNAISE

Low-cal and with the bonus of added protein, it's hard to distinguish this mayonnaise from the real thing. Great for dipping steamed asparagus or in place of regular mayo in potato salad, sandwiches, etc.

1 cup	drained, mashed tofu	250 mL
2 tbsp	vegetable oil	25 mL
1 tbsp	white wine vinegar	15 mL
1 tbsp	lemon juice	15 mL
1 tsp	Dijon mustard	5 mL
	Salt and pepper to taste	

• Process all ingredients in food processor or blender until smooth. Chill.

Makes 1¼ cups (300 mL).

LOW-CAL YOGURT DRESSING

This yummy dressing carried Sun *columnist Karen Boulton through some difficult days of weight loss as she sweetened the pill of salad and cooked skinless chicken breasts with this flavorful dressing.*

1 cup	unflavored low-fat yogurt	250 mL
1 tbsp	Dijon mustard or to taste	15 mL
pinch	mixed dried herbs (dill, thyme, etc.)	pinch
	Artificial sweetener equivalent to	
	½ tsp/2 mL sugar	
	Salt and pepper to taste	

- Whisk all ingredients together in small bowl. Store in fridge in airtight container.

Makes about 1 cup/250 mL.

YOUR BASIC VINAIGRETTE

The first thing my mother taught me to cook, this is an indispensable item in anyone's cooking repertoire. The formula is basically one part vinegar or lemon juice to three parts oil. Try using unusual oils for variety. I like walnut oil the best, but nothing beats a really good extra-virgin olive oil. Purists claim you shouldn't chill olive oil but be sure to keep it in a cool, dark place. If you're making a batch of this vinaigrette to keep in the fridge, bring to room temperature before using.

For a fabulous creamy French vinaigrette, add 1 egg yolk to the vinegar mixture before whisking in the oil.

¼ tsp	salt	1 mL
1 tbsp	red or white wine vinegar	15 mL
1 tbsp	lemon juice	15 mL
¼ tsp	freshly ground black pepper	1 mL
1 tsp	Dijon mustard	5 mL
⅓ cup	olive, nut or other oil	75 mL

- Dissolve salt in vinegar and lemon juice in bowl. Stir in pepper and mustard. Whisk in oil slowly in thin stream until well blended.

Makes ½ cup (125 mL).

NOTE: You can also make this by shaking all ingredients together in a screwtop jar. However, because you have not emulsified the dressing, it will separate and must be shaken again before using.

SOY SAUCE DRESSING

Chef and co-owner of Toronto's Beaujolais restaurant, Bob Bermann, got this unbeatable formula for soy sauce salad dressing from his Aunt Olive. Low in calories and cholesterol, this keeps well in the fridge stored in an airtight container and goes well on almost any combination of fresh veggies.

1	clove garlic, minced	1
1 tbsp	granulated sugar	15 mL
½ cup	cider vinegar	125 mL
½ cup	safflower oil	125 mL
3 tbsp	Kikkoman soy sauce	45 mL
1 tbsp	HP sauce	15 mL

• Combine all ingredients in screwtop jar with tight-fitting lid. Shake well.

Makes about 1⅓ cups/325 mL.

CUCUMBER RAITA

This East Indian salad goes well with curry but is a refreshing accompaniment to roast or barbecued meats of all kinds.

1	large English cucumber	1
2 tbsp	finely chopped onions	25 mL
¼ tsp	salt	1 mL
1 tbsp	chopped fresh coriander	15 mL
1 cup	unflavored yogurt	250 mL
1 tsp	ground cumin	5 mL
	Salt and freshly ground black pepper to taste	

• Peel cucumber, leaving a few strips of peel for color. Slice in half lengthwise. Scoop out seeds with spoon or melon baller. Cut into ¼-inch/5-mm slices.

• Combine sliced cucumber, onions and salt in bowl. Let sit 5 minutes. Drain off liquid.

• Combine coriander, yogurt and cumin in small bowl. Add to cucumber mixture. Add salt and pepper. Chill.

Serves 4 as accompaniment to curry.

ARLENE'S ANCHOVY RED PEPPER SALAD

This by now famous recipe was the star at a memorable meal served by Sun food writers and radio broadcaster Arlene Bynon to four of Toronto's top chefs. Asked to review the meal in an article called "Turning the Tables," these chefs made sure those tables really turned! But all is forgiven, and the whole event made a gripping story. This salad, which Arlene and her husband developed together, is a garlic-lover's dream. An elegant dinner-party appetizer.

4	sweet red peppers	4

• Place peppers on cookie sheet. Broil in oven or grill on barbecue, turning at intervals, until black and blistered on all sides. Place immediately in brown paper bag; twist top to seal. Let sit 10 minutes or until cool enough to handle. Peel off skin with sharp knife; remove core and seeds. Cut in strips ¼ inch/5 mm wide.

DRESSING:

1 tbsp	Dijon mustard	15 mL
3 tbsp	red wine vinegar	45 mL
1	clove garlic, minced	1
1 tbsp	fresh marjoram or 1 tsp/5 mL dried	15 mL
2 tbsp	finely chopped fresh parsley	25 mL
⅔ cup	olive oil	150 mL
	Freshly ground black pepper to taste	

• Whisk together mustard, vinegar, garlic, marjoram and parsley in bowl. Add oil in thin stream, whisking constantly, until well blended. Add black pepper.

8	anchovy fillets	8

• Add slivered red peppers and anchovies to dressing. Let marinate at least 30 minutes.

4	round slices goat's cheese (about ½ inch/ 1 cm thick)	4

• Arrange red peppers in fan shape on four individual plates. Place anchovy strips on top of peppers. Place goat's cheese in centre of fan or as desired. Spoon dressing on top.

Serves 4.

MARINATED VEGGIE SALAD

Susan Mendelson and Deborah Roitberg are two ex-Torontonians who have made their culinary mark in Vancouver with a famous catering/take-out store called Lazy Gourmet. They served this salad to a group of food writers when we were guests of the B.C. Fisheries in the summer of '85.

2 tbsp	sesame seeds	25 mL
¼ cup	red wine vinegar	50 mL
2 tbsp	soy or tamari sauce	25 mL
1	clove garlic, minced	1
1 tsp	grated fresh ginger root	5 mL
1 tsp	granulated sugar	5 mL
¾ cup	olive oil or vegetable oil	175 mL
6 cups	chopped assorted vegetables (blanched cauliflower and broccoli florets, blanched snowpeas, celery, mushrooms, etc.)	1.5 L

• Shaking constantly, toast sesame seeds in heavy skillet over low heat until golden brown, about 5 minutes.
• Whisk together vinegar, soy sauce, garlic, ginger root and sugar in bowl or process in blender until well blended. Add oil in thin stream. Whisk until blended.
• Toss vegetables with dressing and sesame seeds. Chill.

Serves 4.

ASPARAGUS VINAIGRETTE

When asparagus is at its peak in the spring, there's no way I can pass it up. This is one of the simplest and best ways to prepare it. Remember that the tough stalks won't get tender no matter how you cook them, so trim off the ends and peel the bottoms of fat, fibrous asparagus with a potato peeler to ensure that they cook through.

1 lb	fresh asparagus, coarse ends trimmed and fat stalks peeled	500 g

• Lay asparagus flat in large skillet containing a little water. Simmer, covered, until tender, 3 to 4 minutes. Transfer to strainer. Refresh under cold running water. Pat dry with paper towels.
• Arrange on serving platter.

DRESSING:

2 tbsp	white wine or tarragon vinegar	25 mL
½ tsp	Dijon mustard	2 mL
1	clove garlic, minced	1
	Salt and pepper to taste	
1 tbsp	mixed fresh thyme, parsley and chives or	15 mL
	1 tsp/5 mL dried herbs	
¼ cup	olive or vegetable oil	50 mL

- Whisk together all dressing ingredients except oil in bowl or process in blender or food processor until blended. Add oil in thin stream, whisking or processing, until well blended.
- Pour dressing over cooked asparagus. Let marinate a few hours at room temperature.

Serves 4 as side dish.

TURKEY CRANBERRY SALAD

Great made with leftover turkey or chicken. Put any cranberry sauce that lingers after Thanksgiving or Christmas to excellent use this way.

DRESSING:

½ cup	jellied cranberry sauce	125 mL
2 tbsp	olive oil	25 mL
1 tbsp	red or white wine vinegar	15 mL

- Whisk together dressing ingredients in small bowl.

1½ cups	cooked, cubed turkey or chicken	375 mL
½ cup	diced celery	125 mL
1	unpeeled apple, diced	1
3	green onions, chopped	3
¾ cup	seedless grapes, halved	175 mL
	Salt and pepper to taste	
½ cup	chopped walnuts	125 mL
2 tbsp	chopped fresh parsley	25 mL

- Combine turkey, celery, apple, green onions, grapes, salt and pepper in large bowl. Pour dressing over turkey. Refrigerate 1 hour.
- Shaking constantly, toast walnuts in heavy skillet over low heat until aromatic, about 5 minutes. Sprinkle on top of salad. Top with chopped parsley.

Serves 4 as main course.

RHODES' CHINESE CASHEW CHICKEN SALAD

Rhodes' restaurant in Toronto keeps this gorgeous salad on its menu for good reason. A soy ginger marinade, Chinese cabbage and bean sprouts all combine to make one of the best chicken dishes I've tasted.

¼ cup	Hoisin sauce	50 mL
1 tbsp	ketchup	15 mL
1 tbsp	granulated sugar	15 mL
2 tbsp	dry sherry	25 mL
2 tbsp	soy sauce	25 mL
1	clove garlic, minced	1
½ tsp	ground ginger	2 mL
2 tbsp	water	25 mL
6	single boneless chicken breasts	6

• Whisk all ingredients except chicken together in bowl.
• Place chicken breasts in large shallow non-metallic dish big enough to hold them in single layer. (Use two dishes if necessary.) Pour marinade on top. Marinate 6 hours or overnight, turning once.
• Preheat oven to 350°F/180°C.
• Transfer chicken to roasting pan, skin side up. Bake 20 to 30 minutes or until cooked. Cool.

DRESSING:

1	egg	1
2 tbsp	red wine vinegar	25 mL
	Salt and pepper to taste	
2 tbsp	sesame oil	25 mL
¼ cup	vegetable oil	50 mL

• Whisk together egg, vinegar, salt and pepper in small bowl. Combine oils in separate small bowl. Slowly whisk into egg mixture, whisking constantly, until well blended.

½ cup	cashew nuts, coarsely chopped	125 mL
½	head Chinese cabbage, shredded (about 6 cups/1.5 L)	½
1 cup	bean sprouts	250 mL
1	large orange	1
3	green onions, chopped	3

- Shaking constantly, toast cashews in heavy skillet over low heat until golden brown, about 5 minutes. Cool. Place in large bowl. Add cabbage and bean sprouts. Add dressing. Toss.
- Cut orange into segments.
- Slice each chicken breast into 3 or 4 pieces lengthwise. Place one sliced breast on each individual plate. Garnish with orange segments and chopped green onions. Divide cabbage mixture between plates, placing beside chicken. (Or you could serve sliced chicken on one large platter and salad in attractive serving bowl and let people serve themselves.)

Serves 6 as main dish.

LARGE CHICKEN SALAD

Jackie Eddy, food editor of the Edmonton Sun, *recommends this superb salad for summer picnics. So do I. The recipe comes from her third cookbook,* The Second Slice. *In it Eddy describes this dish as "easy to prepare, a prize-winning meal that still leaves time to play 18 holes of golf."*

2 cups	slivered almonds	500 mL
2 ½ cups	mayonnaise	625 mL
1 tbsp	curry powder or to taste	15 mL
1 tbsp	soy sauce	15 mL
8	single cooked chicken breasts, boned, skinned and diced	8
2	10-oz/284-mL cans water chestnuts, drained	2
2 cups	seedless grapes, halved	500 mL
2 cups	sliced celery	500 mL
1	14-oz/398-mL can pineapple chunks, drained	1
2	10-oz/284-mL cans mandarin oranges, drained	2
	Lettuce leaves	

- Shaking constantly, toast almonds in heavy skillet over low heat until golden brown, about 5 minutes.
- Combine mayonnaise, curry powder and soy sauce in large bowl. Add almonds, chicken, water chestnuts, grapes, celery, pineapple and oranges; toss gently. Refrigerate several hours or overnight. Serve on individual plates on a lettuce leaf.

Serves 16.

ORIENTAL CHICKEN SALAD

To poach chicken, follow the method in Avocado Chicken Papaya Salad (page 50). It is guaranteed to produce juicy results. This salad has the crunch of bean sprouts and water chestnuts, the moistness of chicken and the exotic Oriental tang of sesame oil in the dressing. Vary the vegetables as desired.

DRESSING:

1	clove garlic, minced	1
1 tsp	minced fresh ginger root	5 mL
3 tbsp	sesame oil	45 mL
1 tbsp	soy sauce	15 mL
1 tbsp	red wine or tarragon vinegar	15 mL
pinch	granulated sugar	pinch
	Freshly ground black pepper to taste	

• Whisk together dressing ingredients in small bowl until well blended.

4	single chicken breasts, cooked, boned and cut in julienne strips or diced	4
1	small zucchini, cut in julienne strips	1
1	carrot, cut in julienne strips	1
1	sweet red pepper, cut in julienne strips	1
2 cups	bean sprouts	500 mL
1 cup	drained canned water chestnuts, sliced	250 mL
¼ cup	sesame seeds	50 mL
3	green onions, chopped	3
2 tbsp	chopped fresh coriander (optional)	25 mL

• Combine chicken, zucchini, carrot, red pepper, bean sprouts and water chestnuts in large bowl. Pour dressing over salad. Toss.

• Shaking constantly, toast sesame seeds in heavy skillet over low heat until golden brown, about 5 minutes. Sprinkle over salad along with green onions and coriander.

Serves 4.

MALCOLM'S BEEF SALAD

A pasta salad with an Oriental twist from Malcolm MacFarlane, talented Toronto caterer and food stylist. This appeared in "Cold Pasta Is Hot Stuff" in September '85, when pasta salads were the height of food fashion. Luckily the fashion was more than a fad and these salads have become part of many a cooking repertoire. Great in summer as a luncheon entree.

| 8 oz | stout pasta such as fusilli, penne or medium shells (about 3 cups/750 mL) | 250 g |
| 1 tbsp | olive oil | 15 mL |

• Cook pasta in plenty of boiling salted water until al dente. Drain. Toss in bowl with oil. Chill.

1 tsp	butter	5 mL
1 tsp	olive oil	5 mL
8 oz	good-quality beefsteak, cut in paper-thin slices	250 g
1	clove garlic, finely chopped	1
1 tbsp	minced fresh ginger root	15 mL
½	small onion, chopped	½
¼ cup	beef stock	50 mL
1 tsp	honey	5 mL
1 tsp	red wine vinegar	5 mL
½ tsp	Chinese chili sauce or to taste	2 mL

• Heat butter and oil in heavy skillet. Add beef; saute until medium-rare, about 1 minute. Remove from skillet; cool.
• Add garlic, ginger and onion to skillet. Saute until onion has softened, about 5 minutes. Stir in stock, honey, vinegar and chili sauce. Pour into blender or food processor. Blend until smooth. Cool.

4 oz	snow peas (about 1 ½ cups/375 mL)	125 g
1	carrot, cut in julienne strips	1
½	sweet red pepper, cut in julienne strips	½
½	green pepper, cut in julienne strips	½
	Salt to taste	
2 tbsp	sesame oil	25 mL

• Blanch snow peas by plunging into boiling water 30 seconds to 1 minute or until tender-crisp. Refresh under cold running water. Pat dry with paper towels.
• Combine cooked pasta, cooked beef, blended dressing mixture, blanched snow peas and remaining ingredients in large bowl. Toss well. Serve at room temperature.

Serves 4 to 6 as main course.

NOTE: Chinese chili sauce can be found in Chinese groceries and many supermarkets. You can also use Tabasco or your favorite hot sauce to taste.

Avocado Chicken Papaya Salad

A super combination of flavors from Ellen Green, chef at the McGill Club in Toronto, where this is a lunchtime favorite. Use cold roast chicken instead of poached if desired.

DRESSING:

	Grated rind of 1 lime or lemon	
⅓ cup	lime or lemon juice	75 mL
¾ cup	walnut or vegetable oil	175 mL
	Salt and pepper to taste	

- Whisk dressing ingredients together in small bowl until well blended.

6	single chicken breasts	6
	Boston or leaf lettuce	
2	ripe papayas, peeled, seeded and sliced	2
2	ripe avocados, peeled, pitted and sliced	2
½ cup	chopped walnuts	125 mL
	Watercress for garnish	

- Cover chicken with cold water in saucepan with lid. Bring to boil. Reduce heat; simmer, covered, 5 minutes. Remove from heat. Turn chicken over. Let sit, covered, 5 minutes. Remove lid. Let sit 10 minutes. Remove chicken from broth. Remove meat from bones; discard skin and bones. Chill chicken. Cut in slices 1 inch/2 cm wide.
- Line six individual plates with lettuce. Arrange alternate slices of chicken, papaya and avocado on top. Sprinkle with walnuts.
- Drizzle dressing over salad on plates. Garnish with watercress.

Serves 6.

Magic Pan
Orange Almond Salad

This salad, which appeared in Open Kitchen in May, 1985, is definitely the Sun's *most-requested recipe. That made-in-heaven match of oranges and almonds tossed with Romaine lettuce and doused in a creamy vinaigrette is truly magnificent. The idea came from the Magic Pan restaurant via a reader's request. We thank them both.*

¼ cup	sliced almonds	50 mL
1	head Romaine lettuce	1
2	green onions, chopped	2
1	10-oz/284-mL can mandarin oranges, well drained	1

• Shaking constantly, toast almonds in heavy skillet over low heat until golden brown, about 5 minutes.

• Wash and dry lettuce. Tear into bite-sized pieces. Place with green onions and mandarin oranges in large salad bowl.

CREAMY DRESSING:

2 tbsp	granulated sugar	25 mL
	Salt and pepper to taste	
½ tsp	dried tarragon	2 mL
dash	Tabasco sauce	dash
⅓ cup	tarragon vinegar	75 mL
1	egg yolk	1
¾ cup	vegetable oil	175 mL

• Combine sugar, salt, pepper, tarragon and Tabasco in blender or food processor. With machine running, gradually add vinegar, then egg yolk. Add oil in thin stream; process until well blended. Makes about 1 cup/250 mL.

• Just before serving, add desired amount of dressing to salad. Toss well. Sprinkle with toasted almonds.

Serves 6 as side dish.

NOTE: Store any leftover dressing in airtight container in fridge up to 1 week.

MARCEL'S BISTRO SALAD

This salad is typical of the imaginative, flavorful food at Marcel's Bistro—a consistently good place to enjoy French bistro cuisine in Toronto. Chef and co-owner Fabien Siebert wisely keeps this delectable salad on the menu as a lunch and dinner standby.

DRESSING:

¼ cup	milk	50 mL
2 tbsp	red wine vinegar	25 mL
	Salt and pepper to taste	
2 tbsp	grainy (Pommery) mustard	25 mL
¼ cup	olive oil	50 mL
¼ cup	vegetable oil	50 mL

• Whisk together milk, vinegar, salt and pepper in small bowl until well blended. Whisk in mustard. Combine oils and add to dressing in thin stream, whisking constantly, until well blended.

2	single chicken breasts, skin and bones removed	2
pinch	dried thyme	pinch
	Salt and pepper to taste	
1 tbsp	butter	15 mL
½	10-oz/284-g package fresh spinach	½
1	head Boston lettuce	1
1	small head leaf lettuce	1
4 oz	goat's cheese	125 g
12 to 18	thin slices white or dark French stick	12 to 18

• Place chicken between two layers of wax paper. Pound with back of knife or mallet until very thin. Sprinkle with thyme, salt and pepper.

• Heat butter in large skillet. Saute chicken 30 seconds per side or until cooked. Cool. Cut in julienne strips.

• Wash spinach; remove coarse stems. Pat dry with paper towels. Wash lettuce; pat dry. Tear spinach and lettuce into bite-sized pieces and place in large bowl.

• Spread cheese on bread slices. Place on cookie sheet. Cook under broiler until cheese is bubbly, about 2 minutes.

• Add dressing to spinach/lettuce mixture. Toss. Place salad on large platter or individual dinner plates. Place chicken strips on top. Arrange goat's cheese toast rounds around edge of salad.

Serves 4 to 6.

MARION'S PASTA SALAD

This has become one of my favorite summer meals. With the chicken in it, this salad makes a great lunch. Minus the chicken, you've got a super sidekick for barbecued meat or fish. Substitute cooked shrimp, squid or mussels for chicken for a change, or use whatever veggies are in season—go for contrasting colors if possible.

DRESSING:

¼ cup	olive or vegetable oil	50 mL
1 tbsp	soy sauce (optional)	15 mL
2 tbsp	tarragon or wine vinegar	25 mL
1 tsp	Dijon mustard	5 mL
1	clove garlic, minced	1
	Freshly ground black pepper to taste	

• Whisk together dressing ingredients in small bowl until well blended, or shake together in screw-top jar.

8 oz	stout pasta such as fusilli, penne or medium shells (about 3 cups/750 mL)	250 g
1 tbsp	olive or vegetable oil	15 mL

• Cook pasta until al dente in plenty of boiling salted water. Drain. Toss in bowl with oil to prevent sticking. Chill.

2	single chicken breasts	2
1	large sweet red pepper	1
2 cups	broccoli florets, cut in bite-sized pieces	500 mL
1 cup	fresh peas or snow peas	250 mL
¼ cup	pine nuts or slivered almonds	50 mL
¼ cup	chopped fresh parsley or snipped chives	50 mL

• Poach chicken as in Oriental Chicken Salad (page 48). Remove skin and bones. Cut in cubes or julienne strips. Cover; chill.
• Roast red pepper as in Arlene's Anchovy Red Pepper Salad (page 43). Peel, core, seed and cut in julienne strips.
• Steam broccoli and peas until tender-crisp. Refresh under cold water.
• Shaking constantly, toast pine nuts in heavy skillet over low heat until golden brown, about 5 minutes.
• Combine cooked pasta, poached chicken, red peppers, steamed vegetables and dressing in large bowl. Toss. Just before serving, sprinkle salad with parsley and toasted pine nuts.

Serves 4 to 6 as main course.

CRANBERRY CHESTNUT SALAD

This salad is a tradition when Sun *recipe cartoonist, Frances Beaulieu, comes to our house for Thanksgiving or Christmas dinner. It has everything a dish needs to make it special—great looks, texture and taste. It's also easy to make. Make sure the chestnuts are fresh when you buy them—a bad batch could play havoc with your plans.*

1 lb	chestnuts	500 g
3 tbsp	granulated sugar	45 mL
1 ½ cups	fresh cranberries, coarsely chopped	375 mL
3 tbsp	lemon juice	45 mL
1 tsp	Dijon mustard	5 mL
	Salt and freshly ground pepper to taste	
¼ cup	vegetable oil	50 mL
¼ cup	good-quality olive oil	50 mL
3	tart unpeeled apples, cored and cut in bite-sized chunks	3
3	green onions, chopped	3
2	bunches watercress, washed and stems removed	2
	Grated rind of 1 lemon	

• To peel chestnuts, cut an "X" on round side of each chestnut with small sharp knife. Place chestnuts in large saucepan with lid. Add cold water to cover. Bring to boil. Reduce heat; simmer, covered, 20 minutes. Drain. Peel off shells and inner skin, working quickly so chestnuts do not cool. Cut each chestnut into quarters.

• Sprinkle sugar over cranberries in bowl. Toss. Cover. Chill at least 1 hour or overnight.

• Whisk together lemon juice, mustard, salt and pepper in large bowl.

• Combine oils in separate small bowl. Add to lemon juice mixture in thin stream, whisking constantly.

• Add apples, peeled chestnuts and green onions to dressing. Chill at least 1 hour.

• Line attractive serving bowl with watercress. Arrange apple mixture around edge. Spoon cranberries into centre. Sprinkle with lemon rind.

• Serves 6 to 8.

PASTA
AND LIGHT DISHES

BAKED RIGATONI

When I returned from a trip to Italy in 1986, I was eager to share my taste experiences with Sun *readers. To do this, I sought the help of Toronto's pasta pro, Maria Pace, who teaches Italian cooking at hands-on workshops in the heart of Little Italy. In an article called "Don't Leave Rome Without It," I offered Pace's prescription for this hearty dish that can be made ahead or frozen and then re-heated for a quick family meal.*

2 tbsp	butter	25 mL
3 tbsp	olive or vegetable oil	45 mL
1	small onion, finely chopped	1
1	stalk celery, finely chopped	1
1	medium carrot, finely chopped	1
1	clove garlic, minced	1
12 oz	ground veal	375 g
8 oz	ground pork	250 g
1 cup	dry red wine	250 mL
1 cup	chicken or beef stock	250 mL
1	28-oz/796-mL can Italian plum tomatoes, undrained, chopped	1
2 tbsp	tomato paste	25 mL
1 tsp	dried basil	5 mL
	Salt and freshly ground black pepper to taste	
1 lb	rigatoni noodles	500 g
½ cup	freshly grated Parmesan cheese	125 mL
2 cups	grated mozzarella cheese	500 mL

• Heat butter and oil in large heavy saucepan with lid. Add onion, celery and carrot. Saute over medium heat until soft, about 5 minutes. Add garlic; saute over medium heat until softened, about 5 minutes. Add ground meats. Cook a few minutes, stirring, over medium heat until meat loses pink color. Add wine. Bring mixture to boil; cook 1 minute. Add stock, tomatoes, tomato paste and basil. Bring mixture to boil; reduce heat. Simmer, partially covered, about 1½ hours or until thickened. Add salt and pepper. Remove saucepan from heat. Let sit, uncovered, about 20 minutes to mellow flavors.

• Preheat oven to 350°F/180°C.

• Cook rigatoni in plenty of boiling salted water until almost al dente. Drain. Place in bowl. Add half of sauce and ¼ cup/50 mL Parmesan. Toss.

• Place half of rigatoni mixture in 13 × 9-inch/3.5-L ovenproof dish. Top with half of remaining sauce, half of remaining Parmesan and half of mozzarella. Repeat layers, finishing with mozzarella. Bake 30 minutes, uncovered, or until heated through. Brown under broiler a few minutes if desired to crisp top.

Serves 6.

SPAGHETTI CASSEROLE

I knew this dish was a winner when Sun *columnist Karen Boulton, who was testing the recipes for this book, shamefacedly presented me with an almost empty casserole at one of our weekly taste sessions. Her husband, Barney, and one of his friends had made short shrift of this delicious concoction that is sure to be a hit at a pot-luck meal or family dinner.*

8 oz	spaghetti	250 g
2 tbsp	vegetable or olive oil	25 mL
1½ lb	ground beef	750 g
1	14-oz/398-mL can tomato sauce	1
	Salt and pepper to taste	
3 cups	cottage cheese	750 mL
8 oz	cream cheese (room temperature)	250 g
¼ cup	sour cream	50 mL
⅓ cup	chopped green onions	75 mL
½	green pepper, cored, seeded and chopped	½

- Preheat oven to 350°F/180°C.
- Lightly butter 10-cup/2.5-L ovenproof dish.
- Cook spaghetti in plenty of boiling salted water until almost al dente. Drain. Stir in olive or vegetable oil to keep noodles from sticking together. Set aside.
- Saute beef in large heavy skillet just until cooked. Drain off fat. Add tomato sauce, salt and pepper. Remove from heat.
- Combine cottage cheese, cream cheese, sour cream, green onions and green pepper in bowl.
- Spread half of cooked spaghetti in prepared dish. Cover with cheese mixture. Top with remaining spaghetti. Spread tomato/meat mixture on top.
- Bake 45 minutes, uncovered, or until bubbly.

Serves 4 to 6.

NOTE: Can be assembled a day or two ahead and then baked.

PASTA AGLIO E OLIO

Another Italian pasta classic from cooking teacher Maria Pace, in which she adds sun-dried tomatoes (they are optional) to a glorious sauce made with olive oil and garlic. Further proof that simplicity is the key to good cooking as long as you have top-quality ingredients, this recipe calls for the best olive oil (extra virgin, if possible) and really fresh garlic. If you have the time, this is one instance where homemade pasta would make all the difference. Pace prefers to use Romano instead of Parmesan cheese in this for extra bite.

⅔ cup	extra-virgin olive oil	150 mL
2	cloves garlic, finely chopped	2
½ cup	coarsely chopped sun-dried tomatoes	125 mL
¼ cup	water	50 mL
1 lb	spaghetti or other thin pasta	500 g
½ cup	freshly grated Romano or Parmesan cheese	125 mL
	Freshly ground black pepper to taste	

• Heat oil in heavy skillet over medium heat. Add garlic; cook until softened, about 2 minutes. Add tomatoes and water. Simmer gently 5 minutes, stirring occasionally.

• Cook spaghetti in plenty of boiling salted water until al dente. Drain. Transfer to warm serving bowl. Pour on sauce. Toss. Sprinkle with Romano and pepper.

Serves 6 to 8 as side dish or appetizer.

PASTA WITH PESTO

Probably my favorite pasta dish to serve at a barbecue, this is a must in summer when fresh basil is at its best. Make a batch of the pesto sauce and freeze it for winter. (If freezing, omit the nuts and cheese; stir them in before serving.) Use the pesto with pasta, as a garnish for soups or as a superb topping for pizza. The authentic way to make this is with pine nuts, but walnuts also work well. For a zestier flavor, use half Parmesan and half Romano cheese.

2 cups	loosely packed fresh basil leaves	500 mL
2	cloves garlic, peeled	2
¼ cup	pine nuts or walnuts	50 mL
½ cup	freshly grated Parmesan cheese	125 mL
1 cup	good-quality olive oil	250 mL
	Salt and freshly ground black pepper to taste	
1 lb	fettuccine, linguine or other thin pasta	500 g

- Blend basil, garlic, pine nuts and Parmesan in food processor or blender until just mixed. Add oil in thin stream with machine running. Blend until of desired consistency. (It can be smooth or coarse in texture.) Add salt and pepper.
- Cook pasta in plenty of boiling salted water until al dente. Drain. Transfer to warmed serving dish or platter. Pour on pesto sauce. Toss to coat.

Serves 4 to 6.

BONNIE'S PASTA WITH CLAM SAUCE

This recipe appeared in the second article I wrote for the Sun *in November, 1984, in which I asked four of Toronto's top cooks to come up with their favorite quick and easy main course. Cooking teacher and all-round food aficionado Bonnie Stern contributed this recipe, and I've been making it ever since. If you've ever come home from work to find nothing assigned for dinner but have dried pasta and a can of clams on hand, you'll know what a godsend a recipe like this can be!*

⅓ cup	fresh breadcrumbs	75 mL
1 lb	spaghetti or other thin pasta	500 g
½ cup	olive oil	125 mL
4	cloves garlic, finely chopped	4
¼ tsp	hot red pepper flakes or to taste	1 mL
¼ cup	chopped fresh parsley	50 mL
½ cup	dry white wine	125 mL
1	5-oz/142-g can baby clams, undrained	1
	Salt and freshly ground black pepper to taste	

- Toast breadcrumbs in heavy skillet over medium heat until golden brown, about 3 minutes. Set aside.
- Meanwhile, cook pasta in plenty of boiling salted water until al dente. Drain. Transfer to warmed serving dish or platter.
- Heat oil in large heavy skillet or saucepan. Add garlic and pepper flakes. Saute until garlic is tender. Add half the parsley. Add wine. Cook 1 minute. Add clams with juice. Cook 3 minutes or until heated through.
- Pour clam sauce over pasta. Sprinkle with toasted breadcrumbs. Toss. Sprinkle with salt, pepper and remaining parsley.

Serves 4 to 6.

PASTA PRIMAVERA

"Primavera" means "spring" in Italian, and what better dish with which to celebrate the arrival of all those fresh veggies. I offered this idea in an article called "Fasta Pasta," in which I gave ideas for quick meals based on noodles. Use whatever vegetables are in season, making an effort to combine different colors for a stunning presentation.

TOMATO SAUCE:

1 tbsp	olive oil	15 mL
1	small onion, finely chopped	1
2	cloves garlic, finely chopped	2
1	28-oz/796-mL can Italian plum tomatoes, undrained, chopped	1
2 tbsp	fresh basil or 1 tsp/5 mL dried	25 mL
	Salt and freshly ground black pepper to taste	

• Heat oil in heavy saucepan. Add onion and garlic; saute until soft, about 5 minutes. Add tomatoes, basil, salt and pepper. Bring to boil; reduce heat. Simmer, uncovered, 10 minutes. Keep warm.

1 lb	spaghetti, linguine, fusilli or other pasta	500 g
2	medium zucchini, cut in ¼-inch/5-mm diagonal slices	2
8 to 10	asparagus spears, cut in 1-inch/2-cm diagonal slices	8 to 10
1 cup	fresh green beans, cut in 1-inch/2-cm pieces	250 mL
1	stalk broccoli, cut in small florets	1
¾ cup	snow peas, topped, tailed and cut in half diagonally	175 mL
½ cup	fresh peas	125 mL
2 tbsp	chopped fresh parsley	25 mL
⅓ cup	pine nuts, toasted (see page 103)	75 mL
½ cup	freshly grated Parmesan cheese	125 mL

• Cook pasta in plenty of boiling salted water until al dente.
• While pasta is cooking, steam vegetables, one kind at a time, until tender-crisp; drain.
• Place cooked pasta in large serving dish or on platter. Top with tomato sauce and then steamed vegetables. Sprinkle with parsley and toasted pine nuts. Serve Parmesan on side.

Serves 6.

PASTA MARINARA

Necessity being the mother of invention, I created this dish one evening with ingredients I had on hand when friends dropped by unexpectedly. And I've been making it ever since. Substitute fresh tomatoes for canned if it's that time of year, and use whatever seafood takes your fancy. Squid and monkfish work particularly well. If you have fresh herbs such as basil or oregano on hand, all the better.

1 tbsp	olive oil	15 mL
1	small onion, finely chopped	1
2	cloves garlic, finely chopped	2
1	28-oz/796-mL can Italian plum tomatoes, undrained, chopped	1
1 tsp	dried oregano	5 mL
	Salt and freshly ground black pepper to taste	
1 lb	linguine, spaghetti or other pasta	500 g
12	mussels, scrubbed and beards removed	12
8 oz	fresh shrimp, peeled and deveined	250 g
1 lb	firm-fleshed fish fillets (cod, grouper, monkfish, etc.), cut in chunks	500 g
¼ cup	chopped fresh Italian or other parsley	50 mL

• Heat oil in heavy saucepan with lid. Add onion and garlic; saute until softened, about 5 minutes. Add tomatoes, oregano, salt and pepper. Bring to boil; reduce heat. Simmer, uncovered, 10 minutes.

• Cook pasta in plenty of boiling salted water until al dente. Drain. Transfer to large warmed serving bowl or platter.

• Steam mussels in large covered saucepan with a little boiling water until they open, a few minutes. Discard any that don't open.

• Add shrimp and fish to tomato sauce. Cover; simmer 3 to 4 minutes or until fish is opaque and just cooked.

• Top pasta with sauce. Arrange mussels around pasta. Sprinkle with parsley.

Serves 6.

PASTA WITH SPICY TOMATO SAUCE

Sometimes called "all'amatriciana" (from the town of Amatrice near Rome), this fiery sauce for pasta is one of my favorites. You can use ham or pancetta, an Italian cross between ham and bacon, instead of bacon.

6	slices bacon, diced	6
1	medium onion, chopped	1
1 tsp	hot red pepper flakes or to taste	5 mL
1	28-oz/796-mL can Italian plum tomatoes, undrained, finely chopped	1
	Freshly ground black pepper to taste	
1 lb	spaghetti, linguine, fettuccine or other thin pasta	500 g
½ cup	freshly grated Romano or Parmesan cheese	125 mL

• Cook bacon in heavy saucepan until lightly colored but not crisp. Add onion and red pepper flakes. Cook over low heat until onion is softened, about 10 minutes. Add tomatoes. Bring to boil; reduce heat. Simmer, uncovered, about 30 minutes or until thickened, stirring occasionally. Add pepper.

• Cook pasta in plenty of boiling salted water until al dente. Drain. Transfer to warmed serving bowl. Pour on sauce. Toss. Sprinkle with a little Romano. Pass remaining cheese on side.

Serves 4 to 6.

FETTUCCINE ALFREDO

This dish was many people's introduction to Italian food back in the sixties and seventies when whipping cream was all the rage. Even in these days of low-fat, low-cal cuisine, fettuccine Alfredo has held its own because it just plain tastes terrific! Kate Bush, cookbook author, food writer and food stylist, contributed this no-fail version to the Sun food section when she was Cook of the Week.

12 oz	fettuccine	375 g
½ cup	butter	125 mL
1 cup	light cream	250 mL
1 cup	freshly grated Parmesan cheese	250 mL
	Freshly ground pepper to taste	
2 tbsp	finely chopped fresh parsley	25 mL

• Cook fettuccine in plenty of boiling salted water until al dente. Drain. Return to saucepan. Set over low heat. Add 2 tbsp/25 mL butter, a little cream and a few spoonfuls of Parmesan. Toss well. Stir in remaining butter, cream and cheese. Sprinkle with pepper and parsley. Transfer to warmed serving bowl or platter.

Serves 4.

LINGUINE WITH FRESH TOMATO SAUCE

A quick, easy meal that makes superb use of all those fresh tomatoes at harvest time. Trust the people at Foodland Ontario to think of this excellent recipe that barely cooks those succulent tomatoes so they retain flavor and shape, while enhancing them wonderfully with aromatic fresh basil. Make the sauce while the pasta cooks and you've got a meal to remember, in a matter of minutes.

12 oz	linguine, spaghetti or other pasta	375 g
¼ cup	freshly grated Parmesan cheese	50 mL
2 tbsp	butter	25 mL
2 tbsp	olive oil	25 mL
1	medium onion, finely chopped	1
2	cloves garlic, finely chopped	2
6	medium fresh tomatoes, diced	6
¼ cup	chopped fresh basil	50 mL
	Salt and freshly ground pepper to taste	
2 tbsp	chopped fresh parsley	25 mL

• Cook linguine in plenty of boiling salted water until al dente. Drain. Transfer to warmed serving dish. Stir in Parmesan and butter.

• While linguine is cooking, heat oil in heavy saucepan or skillet. Add onion and garlic; saute over medium heat until softened. Stir in tomatoes, basil, salt and pepper. Cook, stirring gently at intervals, just until tomatoes are heated through and still retain shape.

• Spoon cooked linguine onto serving plates. Top with sauce. Sprinkle with parsley.

Serves 4 as main course, 6 as appetizer.

PENNE ALLA VODKA

You could also use spaghetti, linguine or any thin pasta for this gorgeous chili-zapped dish made with a vodka sauce—the brainchild of Ruth Fremes, host of CFTO's excellent cooking show, "What's Cooking with Ruth Fremes." Made with penne, tube-like pasta with ends cut on the diagonal, this is a tradition in many of Rome's restaurants.

¼ cup	vodka	50 mL
1 tbsp	hot red pepper flakes	15 mL
1 lb	penne or other pasta	500 g
2 tbsp	butter	25 mL
1 tbsp	vegetable or olive oil	15 mL
½ cup	chopped onion	125 mL
2	large fresh tomatoes, peeled, seeded and chopped (see page 10)	2
⅓ cup	whipping cream	75 mL
	Salt and pepper to taste	
½ cup	freshly grated Parmesan cheese	125 mL

• Combine vodka and red pepper flakes in small covered container or bowl. Let steep 3 days. Strain; discard red pepper flakes, reserving vodka.

• Cook pasta in plenty of boiling salted water until al dente.

• While pasta is cooking, heat butter and oil in large skillet or saucepan. Add onion; saute until softened, about 5 minutes. Stir in tomatoes. Cook 5 minutes, stirring occasionally. Stir in cream and vodka. Simmer 2 minutes. Add salt and pepper. Spoon a little sauce into large warmed serving dish to coat bottom of dish.

• Drain pasta. Transfer to serving dish. Add remaining sauce. Toss. Sprinkle with a little Parmesan. Pass remaining Parmesan on side.

Serves 6 to 8 as side dish, 4 to 6 as main course.

FETTUCCINE WITH PROSCIUTTO

Umberto Menghi is a well-known Vancouver restaurateur who has also written cookbooks and produces his own line of Italian foods. This is one of his recipes, and a tasty one it is, too.

1 lb	fettuccine or other pasta	500 g
2 tbsp	butter	25 mL
6	slices prosciutto ham, trimmed of fat and cut in strips	6
1½ cups	fresh or frozen, thawed peas	375 mL
1 tsp	white pepper	5 mL

| 1 cup | light cream | 250 mL |
| 1 cup | freshly grated Parmesan cheese | 250 mL |

- Cook fettuccine in plenty of boiling salted water until al dente.
- While pasta is cooking, heat butter in large heavy saucepan or skillet. Add prosciutto. Saute until soft but not crisp. Add peas. Cook a few minutes or until tender but not mushy, stirring occasionally. (Frozen will only take about 1 minute to cook.) Add pepper.
- Drain fettuccine. Add to prosciutto-pea mixture. Add cream. Cook over medium heat, stirring, 1 minute or until cream begins to thicken. Add about ¼ cup/50 mL Parmesan. Toss. Transfer to warmed serving dish. Pass remaining Parmesan on side.

Serves 4 to 6.

PASTA WITH OLIVES

Luigi Orgera, chef and owner of Toronto's La Fenice restaurant, makes some of the most heavenly pasta dishes I've ever tried—and that includes my trip to Italy! This beautiful dish can be put together in a matter of minutes, since you make the sauce while the pasta cooks. Sun-dried tomatoes can be found in Italian grocery stores, gourmet shops and even some supermarkets. Use the best olive oil you can find.

12 oz	spaghetti, linguine or other thin pasta	375 g
2 tbsp	extra-virgin olive oil	25 mL
1	anchovy fillet, finely chopped	1
1	clove garlic, minced	1
1	fresh tomato, peeled, seeded and chopped (see page 10)	1
12	black Italian olives, pitted and halved	12
2	sun-dried tomatoes, cut in strips	2
1 tbsp	chopped fresh parsley	15 mL
4	leaves fresh basil, cut in strips	4
	Freshly ground black pepper to taste	

- Cook spaghetti in plenty of boiling salted water until almost al dente. Drain, reserving ¼ cup/50 mL of its cooking liquid.
- Meanwhile, heat oil in large heavy saucepan. Add anchovy; saute until it dissolves, stirring constantly. Add garlic, tomato, olives and sun-dried tomatoes; saute 1 minute.
- Add reserved liquid and partially cooked pasta to sauce. Cook 1 minute over medium heat, adding a little more water if necessary. Stir in parsley, basil and pepper. Serve at once.

Serves 4.

THE BOY'S SPAGHETTI PERONCINI

When I scoured the Sun *newsroom for recipes to appear in "Fasta Pasta"—an article on how to make a quick meal based on noodles—columnist Christie Blatchford was quick to boast about this creation of her husband, David, better known as "The Boy." He re-created this spaghetti dish with croutons and veggies after the two returned from the south of Italy. Why "peroncini?" "I just liked the sound of it," is The Boy's reply!*

⅓ cup	olive oil	75 mL
2	slices bread, diced	2
2	green peppers, chopped	2
2	cloves garlic, finely chopped	2
3 cups	chopped fresh mushrooms	750 mL
1 lb	spaghetti or other thin pasta	500 g
	Freshly ground black pepper to taste	
1 cup	freshly grated Parmesan cheese	250 mL

• Heat 2 tbsp/25 mL oil in wok or large heavy saucepan. Add bread; saute over medium-high heat until golden brown. Drain on paper towels. Add 2 tbsp/25 mL more oil to saucepan. Add green peppers and garlic. Saute until softened, about 5 minutes. Add mushrooms. Saute 3 minutes.

• Meanwhile, cook pasta in plenty of boiling salted water until al dente. Drain.

• Transfer cooked pasta to wok. Add remaining oil. Toss. Add pepper. Add croutons (fried bread cubes) and ½ cup/125 mL Parmesan. Toss. Pass remaining cheese on side.

Serves 4 to 6 as main course.

GNOCCHI GORGONZOLA

Gnocchi are tiny Italian dumplings for which I have an incredible weakness. You can make your own, but this is a tricky affair that takes practice. The storebought version—fresh, frozen or vacuum-packed—can be found at Italian groceries and works perfectly well. Serve them with a simple tomato sauce made with fresh or canned tomatoes (see Linguine with Fresh Tomato Sauce, page 63) or with this creamy rendition from Toronto's La Bettola restaurant. It has the magnificent zap of that pungent blue cheese from the north of Italy—Gorgonzola.

1 lb	gnocchi	500 g
1 tbsp	butter	15 mL
1	clove garlic, finely chopped	1
¾ cup	whipping cream	175 mL
4 oz	Gorgonzola cheese	125 g
1 tbsp	freshly grated Parmesan cheese	15 mL
	Salt and freshly ground pepper to taste	
2 tbsp	chopped fresh parsley	25 mL

- Bring large pot of salted water to boil. Add gnocchi. Cook 3 to 5 minutes or until gnocchi float to surface. Drain. Set aside.
- Melt butter in saucepan. Add garlic; saute 1 minute. Add cream. Bring to boil. Reduce heat to low. Add Gorgonzola and Parmesan; stir until melted. Add cooked gnocchi, salt, pepper and parsley. Toss together. Serve at once in warmed serving bowl.

Serves 4 as appetizer.

SPAGHETTI WITH BURNT BUTTER

This superb recipe, from Kenneth Peace at The Spaghetti Factory in Toronto, appeared in Open Kitchen in response to a reader's request. And what a dish it is! Mizithra is a Greek cheese available at most grocery stores along Toronto's Danforth strip, but grated Parmesan or Romano will do in a pinch. Almost burning the butter is the secret to this sauce's sweet, simple success.

1 cup	butter	250 mL
1 lb	spaghetti or other thin pasta	500 g
12 oz	mizithra, Parmesan or Romano cheese, grated (about 1½ cups/375 mL)	375 g
	Freshly ground black pepper to taste	

- To clarify butter, melt in heavy saucepan over low heat. Remove from heat. Let sit a few minutes. Milk solids will settle on bottom. Skim foam from surface. Pour into another saucepan, discarding solids that remain.
- Heat clarified butter over low heat 8 to 10 minutes, or until golden brown; watch carefully to make sure it doesn't burn.
- While butter is cooking, cook spaghetti in plenty of boiling salted water until al dente. Drain. Transfer to warmed serving dish or platter. Sprinkle with cheese. Pour on butter. Add pepper. Toss.

Serves 4 to 6 as main course, 6 to 8 as side dish.

LEMONY FETTUCCINE WITH FRESH ASPARAGUS

When homegrown fresh asparagus signals the arrival of spring, I'm always on the lookout for new ways to use that most amazing of vegetables. Nothing beats eating it freshly steamed and dipped in lemony mayonnaise. But this creation from co-chefs Keith Froggett and Daniel Villet of Scaramouche restaurant in Toronto comes a close second. They recommend using fresh egg noodles, but the results will be good even if you use dried. If using homemade chicken stock, reduce it by boiling it down until it's really full-bodied.

This recipe could be adapted by omitting the asparagus and adding ¼ cup/50 mL chopped fresh dill to make a superb lemony dill sauce.

1 lb	fresh green asparagus	500 g
1 lb	fettuccine, linguine or other thin pasta	500 g
1 tbsp	butter	15 mL
1	clove garlic, finely chopped	1
1 tsp	minced shallot or onion	5 mL
1 cup	full-bodied chicken stock	250 mL
1 cup	whipping cream	250 mL
¼ cup	lemon juice	50 mL
½ cup	freshly grated Parmesan cheese	125 mL
	Salt and freshly ground white pepper to taste	

• Peel outer layer from any thick asparagus stalks with vegetable peeler. Snap off tough ends. Cut into ½-inch/1-cm pieces on the diagonal. Blanch by cooking in pot of boiling water until tender-crisp, 1 to 2 minutes. Drain.

• Cook pasta in plenty of boiling salted water until al dente.

• While pasta is cooking, heat butter in heavy skillet or saucepan. Add garlic and shallot; saute until soft, about 2 minutes. Add chicken stock. Bring to boil; reduce heat. Simmer 1 to 2 minutes. Add cream, lemon juice and Parmesan. Bring to boil; reduce heat. Simmer, stirring, until slightly thickened, about 2 minutes. Add cooked asparagus, salt and pepper. Toss.

• Drain pasta. Transfer to warmed serving dish or platter. Pour on sauce. Toss.

Serves 4 to 6.

NOODLES WITH WILD MUSHROOM SAUCE

Porcini are wild mushrooms that are a popular delicacy in Italy. The dried ones work wonderfully in this easy-to-make pasta sauce from Italian cooking teacher Maria Pace. The mushrooms can be found in most Italian grocery stores and some supermarkets at a surprisingly reasonable price.

2	14-g packages dried wild mushrooms (e.g. porcini)	2
1½ cups	hot water	375 mL
½ cup	vegetable oil	125 mL
3 tbsp	finely chopped shallots or onion	45 mL
1	clove garlic, minced	1
	Salt to taste	
1 lb	linguine, fettuccine or other pasta	500 g
3 tbsp	butter	45 mL
¾ cup	freshly grated Parmesan cheese	175 mL

• Soak mushrooms in hot water 30 minutes or until soft. Strain mushrooms through sieve lined with damp cheesecloth, J-cloth or paper towel to remove grit. Reserve liquid. Rinse mushrooms and pat dry.

• Heat oil in large heavy skillet or saucepan. Add shallots; saute until softened, about 5 minutes. Add mushrooms, reserved soaking liquid and garlic. Add salt. Simmer 10 minutes.

• While sauce is cooking, cook pasta in plenty of boiling salted water until al dente. Drain. Transfer to warmed serving dish or platter.

• Add butter to mushroom sauce. Stir until melted. Pour sauce over cooked pasta. Sprinkle on a little Parmesan. Toss. Pass remaining Parmesan on side.

Serves 4 to 6 as main course.

SPAGHETTI ALLA CARBONARA

This dish, an upscale pasta with bacon and eggs, was reputedly the invention of coal miners in the Tuscany region of Italy. It really is a classic and has few equals when done right. It is crucial to toss the hot pasta with the raw eggs as soon as the pasta is cooked, since this is all the cooking the eggs will get. Serve immediately, as the dish loses its character if lukewarm. Pancetta, an Italian cross between bacon and ham, is the authentic ingredient, but lean bacon works perfectly well.

1 lb	spaghetti or other thin pasta	500 g
3 tbsp	vegetable oil	45 mL
4 oz	pancetta or bacon, diced	125 g
2	cloves garlic, finely chopped	2
3 tbsp	butter	45 mL
½ cup	freshly grated Romano cheese	125 mL
1	egg	1
2	egg yolks	2
	Freshly ground black pepper to taste	

• Cook pasta in plenty of boiling salted water until al dente.

• While pasta is cooking, heat oil in large heavy skillet or saucepan. Add pancetta; cook over medium heat a few minutes or until slightly colored. Add garlic; cook 1 minute. Add butter; cook, stirring, until melted.

• In large warmed bowl combine 3 tbsp/45 mL Romano, egg and egg yolks.

• Drain pasta. Add to cheese-egg mixture. Toss. Add pancetta mixture. Toss. Sprinkle with a little more Romano and black pepper. Pass remaining Romano on side.

Serves 4 to 6.

SUMMER PICNIC PIE

A terrific layered omelette-en-croute, this is ideal for picnics or a patio lunch in summer. It involves quite a bit of chopping but is well worth the effort. Serve with a green salad and some chilled white wine. Use cooked spinach or sweet peppers in this if desired.

OMELETTE:

6	eggs, beaten	6
1	green onion, chopped	1
	Salt and pepper to taste	
2 tbsp	butter	25 mL

- Beat eggs, onion, salt and pepper in bowl.
- Heat 1 tbsp/15 mL butter in 8-inch/20-cm heavy skillet over medium heat. Add half of egg mixture, tilting pan so mixture covers bottom. Cook until egg is barely set. Slide omelette onto plate. Repeat with remaining butter and egg mixture to make second omelette.

VEGETABLE LAYER:

2 tbsp	olive or vegetable oil	25 mL
1	clove garlic, finely chopped	1
1	green pepper, seeded and sliced	1
1	medium zucchini, sliced	1
1	medium onion, chopped	1
½ tsp	dried basil	2 mL
½ tsp	dried tarragon	2 mL
2 tbsp	chopped fresh parsley	25 mL
	Salt and pepper to taste	

- Heat oil in heavy skillet. Add remaining ingredients. Saute until vegetables have softened, about 5 minutes. Turn into strainer and drain while preparing pastry.

PASTRY:

1 lb	frozen puff pastry, thawed or fresh	500 g

- Roll out pastry into circle big enough to fit bottom and sides of 9-inch/23-cm springform pan, leaving 4½ inches/10 cm hanging over edges. (Overhanging dough will be used to fold over filling and make top crust for pie.) Prick bottom of dough with fork.

HAM AND CHEESE LAYER:

8 oz	sliced ham or cooked, sliced sausages	250 g
8 oz	sliced Jarlsberg, Swiss or other mild cheese	250 g
2	tomatoes, sliced	2
1	egg, beaten	1

- Preheat oven to 425°F/220°C.
- Layer half each of ham, cheese, vegetables and tomatoes in dough-lined pan. Top with one omelette. Season with salt and pepper. Repeat layer. Fold pastry over filling so edges meet in centre. Decorate with any leftover trimmings of dough if desired, making leaves or flowers. Brush with beaten egg.
- Bake 10 minutes. Reduce heat to 375°F/190°C. Bake 35 minutes or until golden brown. Serve hot or cold.

Serves 8 to 12.

SPAGHETTI ORIENTALI

Talented chef and co-owner of Toronto's Cibo restaurant, Massimo Calovini, created this dish for "Use Your Noodles," in which I asked four restaurateurs to do their stuff with a package of spaghetti. This amazingly simple creation, with the crunch of veggies and the zap of curry powder, is also amazingly good.

1 lb	spaghetti or other thin pasta	500 g
¾ cup	good-quality olive oil	175 mL
1	clove garlic, finely chopped	1
1	anchovy fillet, finely chopped	1
20	snow peas, cut in julienne strips	20
½	small red onion, sliced	½
1 lb	baby shrimp, peeled and deveined	500 g
15	green or black olives, pitted and halved	15
2	green onions, cut in 1-inch/2-cm pieces	2
15	cherry tomatoes, halved	15
1 tsp	curry powder or to taste	5 mL
½ cup	freshly grated Parmesan cheese	125 mL

• Cook pasta in plenty of boiling salted water until al dente. Drain. Keep warm.

• Meanwhile, heat ¼ cup/50 mL oil in large heavy skillet. Add garlic; cook over medium heat until soft. Do not brown. Add anchovy, snow peas, red onion, shrimp, olives and green onions. Cook 2 minutes or until shrimp is pink and curled.

• Add tomatoes and curry powder to shrimp mixture. Stir-fry 1 minute. Add cooked pasta and remaining oil. Toss. Transfer to warmed serving dish or platter. Sprinkle with Parmesan.

Serves 4 to 6.

PASTA PUTTANESCA

"Feeding Bawdy and Soul," a Valentine's article in which I offered food for lovers only, was the obvious spot to feature pasta puttanesca, which means "whore's pasta" in Italian. Perhaps it's the spicy flavor or the fact that this dish takes minutes to make that explains its name. Whatever the semantics, it is an olive/anchovy-lover's dream!

2 tbsp	olive oil	25 mL
2	cloves garlic, finely chopped	2
1	stalk celery, finely chopped	1

1	28-oz/796-mL can Italian plum tomatoes, undrained, finely chopped	1
5	anchovy fillets, finely chopped	5
¼ cup	sliced pimiento-stuffed green olives	50 mL
¼ cup	sliced pitted black olives	50 mL
2 tsp	capers	10 mL
1 tsp	dried basil	5 mL
½ tsp	hot red pepper flakes or to taste	2 mL
	Freshly ground black pepper to taste	
1 lb	spaghetti or other thin pasta	500 g
½ cup	freshly grated Parmesan cheese	125 mL

• Heat oil in heavy saucepan. Add garlic and celery; saute until softened, about 5 minutes. Add tomatoes and anchovies. Bring to boil; reduce heat. Simmer 10 minutes. Stir in olives, capers, basil and pepper flakes. Simmer, uncovered, 20 minutes. Add pepper.

• Meanwhile, cook pasta in plenty of boiling salted water until al dente. Drain. Transfer to warmed serving dish or platter. Top or toss with sauce. Pass Parmesan on side.

Serves 4 to 6.

BEER CHEDDAR FONDUE

This recipe for a new twist on an old theme appeared in a fondue article called "The 'Eat Is On." The combination of beer and Cheddar is first rate. Serve with bite-sized chunks of crusty French bread, raw veggies and apple sections.

1 lb	old Cheddar cheese, grated (about 4 cups/ 1 L)	500 g
1 cup	beer	250 mL
½ tsp	Worcestershire sauce	2 mL
½ tsp	paprika	2 mL
1 tbsp	Dijon mustard	15 mL
pinch	cayenne pepper	pinch
	Salt and freshly ground pepper to taste	

• Combine Cheddar and beer in fondue pot on stove. Heat over low heat, stirring, until melted and well blended. Stir in remaining ingredients.

• Transfer pot from stove to warming stand. Serve with bread chunks, raw veggie dippers or apple sections.

Serves 4.

SPICY SHANGHAI NOODLES

A reader requested this recipe for "mee goreng bandung" from Toronto's Malaysian restaurant, Ole Malacca. Are we glad she did. The combination of tender Shanghai noodles (available fresh in Chinatown), crunchy bean sprouts, juicy shrimp and chicken, all doused in a chili-zapped sauce, is nothing short of sublime.

1 lb	fresh Shanghai egg noodles	500 g
⅓ cup	vegetable oil	75 mL
2	medium boneless, skinless chicken breasts (about 8 oz/250 g), cut in bite-sized pieces	2
8 oz	baby shrimp, peeled and deveined	250 g
1	small bok choy, sliced	1
3	eggs, beaten	3
2 tsp	Chinese chili paste or sauce, or to taste	10 mL
3 tbsp	oyster sauce	45 mL
1 tbsp	soy sauce	15 mL
8 oz	bean sprouts (about 3 cups/750 mL)	250 g
	Lemon wedges for garnish	
	Fresh coriander sprigs for garnish (optional)	

• Cook noodles in plenty of boiling salted water until al dente, about 30 seconds. Drain. Toss with 2 tbsp/25 mL vegetable oil. Keep warm.

• Heat remaining oil in wok or large heavy saucepan over medium-high heat. Add chicken, shrimp and bok choy. Stir-fry 1 minute. Add eggs. Stir-fry 1 minute. Add cooked noodles, chili paste, oyster sauce and soy sauce. Stir-fry 3 minutes more. Add bean sprouts. Toss, cooking just until heated through. Serve at once on warmed serving platter garnished with lemon wedges and coriander sprigs if desired.

Serves 4 to 6.

FOUR SEASONS' VEGETABLE LATKES

This variation on the traditional potato latke makes a great luncheon dish. The recipe comes from Toronto's Four Seasons Hotel, Yorkville.

4	medium potatoes, peeled and grated	4
	Salt for sprinkling	
2	medium onions, finely chopped	2
1	large carrot, peeled and grated	1
1	clove garlic, minced	1
2	eggs, lightly beaten	2
¼ cup	chopped fresh parsley	50 mL
¼ tsp	freshly grated nutmeg	1 mL
	Salt and pepper to taste	
	Oil for frying	

- Lightly sprinkle potatoes with salt. Let sit in strainer 5 minutes. Pat dry with paper towels.
- Combine potatoes, onions, carrot, garlic, eggs, parsley, nutmeg, salt and pepper in bowl. Mix well. Shape into 8 uniform patties.
- Cover bottom of large skillet with thin layer of oil. Heat over medium-high heat. Add latkes. Cook in batches if necessary, 3 to 4 minutes per side or until golden brown. Serve with sour cream or unflavored yogurt.

Serves 4 to 6.

COTTAGE CHEESE PANCAKES

It's easy to become addicted to these protein-packed, low-cal pancakes made from cottage cheese. I got the recipe from my mother and now eat them regularly topped with homemade apple sauce and slightly sweetened plain yogurt.

1 cup	cottage cheese	250 mL
2	eggs	2
2 tbsp	natural bran	25 mL
¼ cup	wholewheat or all-purpose flour	50 mL
pinch	ground cinnamon (optional)	pinch
	Sunflower, safflower, soybean or corn oil	
	for frying	

- Blend cottage cheese and eggs in food processor or blender until smooth. Transfer to bowl. Mix in bran, flour and cinnamon if using.
- Add only enough oil to heavy skillet to barely coat bottom. Heat over medium heat. Add batter by large spoonfuls. Cook until golden brown on one side. Turn pancakes over. Cook other side until golden brown.

Makes 8 to 10.

CREAM CHEESE SOUFFLÉ

When the Sun *food section re-created a "Ladies Lunch," I recruited four female friends to provide the recipes. In full forties regalia, these ladies sat down to one of the tastiest meals I have eaten. This dish came from Polly Evans, who can do wonders with all things meatless. Light, flavorful and a snap to make, this soufflé has only one drawback—it must be whipped up at the last minute to arrive at the table in all its puffed-up glory. Perfect for lunch or brunch, it goes well with a green salad, plenty of crusty bread and, of course, lashings of chilled white wine!*

1 lb	cream cheese (room temperature)	500 g
¼ cup	sour cream or unflavored yogurt	50 mL
1 tbsp	honey	15 mL
2 tsp	chopped chives or green onions	10 mL
3	eggs, separated	3
	Salt and pepper to taste	
½ tsp	cream of tartar	2 mL

- Preheat oven to 350°F/180°C.
- Lightly butter 6-cup/1.5-L soufflé dish.
- Blend cream cheese, sour cream, honey, chives and egg yolks in food processor or blender. Blend 1 minute or until smooth. Mix in salt and pepper. Transfer to large bowl.
- Beat egg whites and cream of tartar in bowl until stiff but not dry. Fold into cream cheese mixture. Turn into prepared dish.
- Bake 30 minutes or until puffed and golden. Centre should still be slightly soft.

Serves 3 to 4 as main course, 4 to 6 as part of brunch buffet.

NACHO PIE

I got this nifty snack idea at the Food Media Conference in New York in January, 1987. A terrific change from pizza and even easier to make.

2	eggs	2
1	210-g package tortilla chips, finely crushed (about 2 cups/500 mL when crushed)	1
12 oz	Monterey Jack cheese, grated	375 g
1	12-oz/341-mL jar mild or medium chunky-style Mexican salsa	1
½ cup	thinly sliced green pepper	125 mL

- Preheat oven to 400°F/200°C.
- Lightly butter 12-inch/30-cm pizza pan.
- Beat eggs in large bowl. Add crushed tortilla chips. Mix well. Press mixture evenly onto pizza pan. Bake 10 minutes. Transfer pan to wire rack. Sprinkle with half of cheese. Spoon salsa on top. Sprinkle with green pepper and remaining cheese. Bake about 3 minutes or until cheese is melted. Serve cut in wedges.

Serves 6 as snack.

OMELETTE SOUFFLÉ NORMANDE

Peggy Murray, entertainment copy editor at the Sun, is an aficionado of good food. She came back with this idea after a trip to France. Calvados, a magnificent apple brandy from Normandy, is essential for the flavor of this dish, which makes an elegant, quick dessert.

4	egg yolks	4
½ cup	granulated sugar	125 mL
pinch	salt	pinch
6	egg whites	6
2 tbsp	unsalted butter	25 mL
½ cup	whipping cream	125 mL
⅓ to ½ cup	Calvados or apple brandy	75 to 125 mL

- Preheat oven to 400°F/200°C.
- In large bowl, beat egg yolks, ¼ cup/50 mL sugar and salt together until light and creamy.
- Beat egg whites in separate bowl until stiff peaks form. Fold into yolk mixture.
- Melt butter in large heavy skillet with metal handle (it will go in oven) over medium-high heat. Heap in egg mixture. Smooth top evenly with spatula. Make several deep cuts in surface with spatula. Cook 1 minute to brown bottom.
- Place in oven 5 minutes or until golden brown.
- While omelette is cooking, whip cream and remaining sugar in bowl with a dash of Calvados. Chill.
- Heat remaining Calvados in small saucepan. Quickly bring it and omelette in skillet to table. Sprinkle on warmed Calvados. Ignite to flambé. Serve with Calvados/whipped cream mixture.

Serves 4.

TOFU EGGPLANT LASAGNA

What a terrific vegetarian way to get your protein. Even meat-eaters, however, will love this dish, which appeared in an article called "Cooking on a Shoestring," in which I offered budget recipes that were tasty to boot.

1	medium eggplant, peeled and sliced about ¼ inch/5 mm thick	1
	Salt for sprinkling	
3 tbsp	vegetable or olive oil	45 mL
1	14-oz/398-mL can tomato sauce, or 1¾ cups/425 mL homemade	1
2	cloves garlic, minced	2
1 tsp	dried basil or 1 tbsp/15 mL chopped fresh	5 mL
1 tsp	dried oregano or 1 tbsp/15 mL chopped fresh	5 mL
	Salt and pepper to taste	
2	medium tomatoes, sliced	2
12	mushrooms, sliced	12
1	medium onion, sliced	1
1 lb	tofu, cut in thin lasagna-like slices	500 g
1 lb	ricotta cheese	500 g
½ cup	grated Parmesan cheese	125 mL
1½ cups	grated mozzarella cheese	375 mL

- Preheat broiler.
- Sprinkle eggplant lightly with salt. Let sit 5 minutes. Pat dry with paper towels to remove bitterness.
- Pour oil in bottom of large shallow ovenproof dish. Arrange eggplant on top in single layer. It may be necessary to do this in several batches. Broil 1 to 2 minutes per side or until golden brown. Transfer to plate.
- Preheat oven to 375°F/190°C.
- Combine tomato sauce, garlic, basil, oregano, salt and pepper in bowl. Pour about ¼ cup/50 mL of sauce into bottom of 13 × 9-inch/3.5-L ovenproof dish. Top with a layer of broiled eggplant, then half each of tomato slices, mushrooms, onion, tofu, tomato sauce and cheeses. Repeat.
- Bake, covered with lid or foil, 30 minutes. Remove lid or foil. Bake 15 minutes more or until bubbly and brown.

Serves 6 to 8.

GUILT-FREE FALAFEL

When I went on my public diet in January, 1985 (I lost seventeen pounds and learned a lot about nutrition and weight control—all of which I wrote about, week by week for six months), Karen Boulton launched a Low-Cal Recipe Contest in Open Kitchen. Inge Gregusch was its winner with this excellent idea for a falafel that is tops in taste and low in calories.

¼ cup	sesame seeds	50 mL
1	10-oz/284-g package fresh spinach	1
3	eggs, beaten	3
2 cups	bean sprouts, coarsely chopped	500 mL
1½ cups	grated carrots	375 mL
¼ cup	all-purpose flour	50 mL
1	small onion, peeled and diced	1
1	clove garlic, minced	1
1 tsp	salt	5 mL
1½ tsp	ground cumin	7 mL
1 tsp	dried oregano	5 mL
½ tsp	freshly ground black pepper	2 mL
¼ tsp	cayenne pepper	1 mL
3	rounds of pita bread	3
2	medium tomatoes, sliced	2
¾ cup	unflavored low-fat yogurt	175 mL
	Chopped fresh parsley for garnish	

• Shaking constantly, toast sesame seeds in heavy skillet over low heat until golden brown, about 5 minutes.

• Wash spinach; remove coarse stems. Do not dry. Place in large saucepan with tight-fitting lid. Steam over medium heat in water that clings to leaves a few minutes until limp. Squeeze dry; chop finely.

• Combine chopped spinach, eggs, bean sprouts, carrots, flour and toasted sesame seeds in bowl. Mix well. Add onion, garlic and seasonings. Mix well.

• Drop mixture in six large spoonfuls into non-stick skillet, patting down gently to form patties. Cook over medium-high heat about 3 minutes per side or until browned.

• To serve, cut top off each pita. Stuff each one with two falafel patties, a couple of tomato slices, a spoonful of yogurt and some chopped parsley.

Serves 3.

MEDITERRANEAN STUFFED BREAD

Make this delectable picnic bread with your favorite crusty round loaf—Italian white, Portuguese cornbread or Russian rye. The Mediterranean flavors of anchovies, olives and tomatoes make perfect summer fare, especially when eaten outdoors and washed down with some hearty red wine.

2	ripe tomatoes, coarsely chopped	2
1 cup	green olives stuffed with pimientos	250 mL
1 cup	pitted black olives	250 mL
2 tbsp	finely chopped red onion	25 mL
3	anchovy fillets, finely chopped (optional)	3
2	cloves garlic, minced	2
3 tbsp	finely chopped fresh basil or oregano or 1 tsp/5 mL dried	45 mL
¼ cup	finely chopped fresh parsley	50 mL
3 tbsp	olive oil	45 mL
2 tbsp	freshly grated Parmesan cheese	25 mL
	Freshly ground black pepper to taste	
1	round loaf crusty bread	1
4 oz	thinly sliced cooked ham	125 g
4 oz	thinly sliced spicy salami	125 g
4 oz	thinly sliced mozzarella, Monterey Jack, Swiss or mild white Cheddar cheese	125 g

• Add tomatoes and olives to food processor. Pulse on/off a few times until coarsely chopped. (You can do this by hand if desired.) Place mixture in strainer; gently press out liquid. Discard liquid. Transfer mixture to bowl with onion, anchovies, garlic, basil, parsley, oil, Parmesan and pepper. Stir to combine.

• Cut top off bread. Scoop out centre, leaving shell 1 inch/2 cm thick. (Save leftover bread for breadcrumbs, poultry stuffing, etc.)

• Spoon half of olive mixture into hollowed loaf. Make alternate layers of ham, salami and cheese until ingredients are used up. Cover with remaining olive mixture. Replace top on bread. Wrap in foil. Place weight (e.g. large can of food) on top of bread. Refrigerate 1 hour. Cut in wedges to serve.

Serves 6.

MEAT AND SEAFOOD

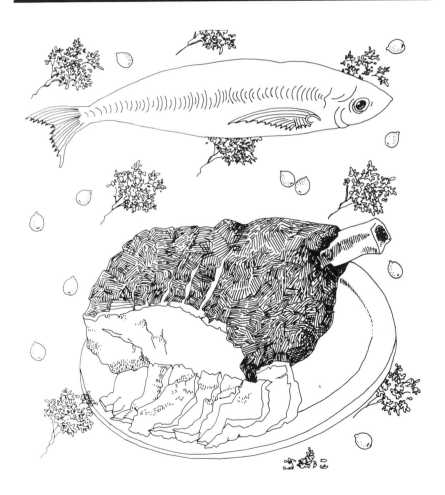

DINI'S BREADALBANE BURGERS

TV personality Dini Petty won a Consumers' Gas Celebrity Cookout in the summer of '85 with this intriguing burger creation. She invented it at her Georgian Bay cottage one summer to commemorate a memorable trip by friend Jo MacGinnis to the Arctic to salvage the ship, the Breadalbane. *These burgers are pretty memorable themselves. The gorgeous red pepper sauce can also be used with pasta and is magnificent with barbecued chicken or fish.*

RED PEPPER SAUCE:

1	medium onion, sliced	1
1 tbsp	olive oil	15 mL
1	clove garlic, minced	1
4 to 5	sweet red peppers, cored, seeded and coarsely chopped	4 to 5
pinch	cayenne pepper	pinch
1 tbsp	lemon juice	15 mL
½ tsp	dried thyme	2 mL
	Salt to taste	

• Place all ingredients except thyme and salt in heavy saucepan with lid. Simmer, covered, about 45 minutes, stirring occasionally. Add thyme just before end of cooking time. Blend mixture in food processor or blender until smooth. Press through sieve to remove skins. Add salt. Keep warm. (Sauce can be made ahead and re-heated.)

BURGERS:

1 tbsp	butter	15 mL
¼ cup	chopped onions	50 mL
1½ lb	lean ground beef	750 g
¼ cup	breadcrumbs	50 mL
2 tbsp	chopped fresh basil	25 mL
1 tsp	olive oil	5 mL
1	egg, lightly beaten	1
	Salt and freshly ground pepper to taste	

• Heat butter in small skillet. Add onions; saute until softened, about 5 minutes.
• Combine remaining ingredients in bowl. Add cooked onions. Mix well. Divide mixture into 4 to 6 uniform patties. Grill on barbecue or under broiler until cooked to desired degree of doneness.
• Spoon sauce on warmed serving platter. Place burgers on top. Serve extra sauce in sauceboat.

Serves 4 to 6.

BARBECUED LAMB STEPHANIE

Radio show host, food critic and food aficionado Jeremy Brown was the runner-up in the Consumers' Gas Celebrity Cookout in the summer of 1985 with this dish. It is worth splurging on the rather pricey butterflied boned leg of lamb that is the crucial ingredient. A great barbecue dish when entertaining.

MARINADE:

3 to 4	large shallots or 1 small onion, peeled	3 to 4
2 tbsp	fresh tarragon or 1 tbsp/15 mL dried	25 mL
1 tbsp	fresh thyme or 1 tsp/5 mL dried	15 mL
1 tbsp	fresh oregano or 1 tsp/5 mL dried	15 mL
1 tbsp	Dijon mustard	15 mL
1 tbsp	grainy (Pommery) mustard	15 mL
	Freshly ground black pepper to taste	
¼ cup	olive oil	50 mL

• Blend all marinade ingredients except oil in food processor or blender until smooth. Add oil in thin stream. Process until well blended. Place in large, shallow non-metallic dish.

5 to 6 lb	boned and butterflied fresh or frozen and thawed leg of lamb	2.5 to 3 kg
5 to 6	unpeeled cloves garlic, crushed	5 to 6

• Place lamb in dish with marinade. It must have room to spread out so marinade permeates meat. Let marinate at least 6 hours or overnight in fridge, turning occasionally.

• Remove lamb from marinade; reserve marinade. Place lamb on barbecue grill over medium-high heat. Place garlic cloves on coals. Close lid of barbecue. Grill lamb 6 to 7 minutes, basting with marinade at intervals. Open lid. Continue cooking 7 to 8 minutes. Turn meat over. Repeat, cooking 6 to 7 minutes with lid closed and 7 to 8 minutes with lid open and basting at intervals. (This will result in rare meat.) Cook longer if desired.

Serves 8 to 10.

BASIC BARBECUED RIBS

If none of the commercial barbecue sauces make the grade in your books, try this gas barbecue recipe on your next batch of ribs, chicken, or any barbecued meat, for that matter.

BARBECUE SAUCE:

¼ cup	butter	50 mL
1	onion, finely chopped	1
1	clove garlic, finely chopped	1
1¼ cups	chili sauce	300 mL
3 tbsp	cider vinegar or lemon juice	45 mL
2 tbsp	Worcestershire sauce	25 mL
½ tsp	dry mustard	2 mL
½ tsp	chili powder	2 mL
½ tsp	ground cumin	2 mL

• Melt butter in medium saucepan. Add onion and garlic; saute until soft. Add remaining ingredients. Bring to boil. Reduce heat; simmer 15 minutes, stirring occasionally.

4 lb	meaty pork spareribs	2 kg
	Vegetable oil for brushing	

• Brush ribs with a little oil. Grill on barbecue over high heat 5 minutes per side to sear meat. Remove from grill. Cover grill with layer of heavy foil punctured with a few holes for ventilation. Place ribs on foil. Brush generously with sauce. Close lid on barbecue. Reduce heat to low. Grill ribs, turning every 15 minutes and basting at intervals with sauce, 45 minutes or until juices run clear when pierced.

Serves 4 to 6.

CAP'S RIBS

Sun columnist Karen Boulton discovered this unbelievable rib recipe at a restaurant in Puerto Plata in the Dominican Republic. If you have leftover sauce, store it in an airtight container in the fridge.

1 cup	water	250 mL
1 tbsp	vinegar	15 mL
1	large onion, cut into slices ¼ inch/5 mm thick	1
4 lb	meaty pork spareribs	2 kg

- Preheat oven to 350°F/180°C.
- Combine water and vinegar in small bowl.
- Arrange onions in single layer in large roasting pan. Place ribs on top. Pour enough water/vinegar mixture over ribs to barely cover bottom of pan. Cover pan with foil. Bake 2½ to 3 hours or until meat is tender, turning a few times and adding extra water/vinegar mixture if necessary to keep bottom of pan covered.

BARBECUE SAUCE:

½ cup	barbecue sauce	125 mL
½ cup	ketchup	125 mL
1 tsp	Worcestershire sauce	5 mL
2 tbsp	honey	25 mL
½ tsp	Tabasco sauce or to taste	5 mL
	Salt and pepper to taste	

- Combine sauce ingredients in small bowl. Mix well.
- Remove ribs from pan. Discard onions and liquid. Cut into single ribs. Return to pan. Brush sauce generously over ribs.
- Broil or grill ribs on barbecue over medium heat, basting with sauce at intervals, 2 to 3 minutes per side or until crisp.

Serves 4 to 6.

CHEATER'S BARBECUED RIBS

Rib purists may fault me for taking the easy route with this recipe. However, my family has been enjoying ribs cooked this way for more barbecue seasons than I can count. Serve them with some pasta doused in pesto (page 58), a crisp green salad and crusty bread.

4 lb	meaty pork spareribs	2 kg
	Favorite homemade (see page 84) or	
	storebought barbecue sauce for brushing	

- Cut ribs in serving-sized portions of 5 to 6 ribs per person. Place in large heavy saucepan. Add just enough water to cover. Bring to boil. Reduce heat; simmer, covered, 30 to 40 minutes or until tender. Drain.
- Place ribs on barbecue grill over medium heat. Brush generously with barbecue sauce. Grill about 5 minutes per side or until crisp, basting at intervals.

Serves 4 to 6.

PORK TENDERLOIN SUN STYLE

The Pork Producers' Marketing Board came up with this recipe for an article I wrote in 1986 called "Tender Is the Loin." I rate pork tenderloin as one of the best meat buys around. Stuffed with dried fruit, it makes an elegant, tasty main course served with noodles and salad.

1 cup	mixed dried fruit	250 mL
1 cup	water	250 mL
2	pork tenderloins (about 12 oz/375 g each)	2
2 cups	fresh bread cubes	500 mL
1 tbsp	chopped fresh parsley	15 mL
¼ tsp	salt	1 mL
¼ tsp	lemon pepper or pepper	1 mL
6	slices bacon	6
¼ cup	dry white vermouth or ¼ cup/50 mL plus 1 tsp/5 mL lemon juice	50 mL

• Bring fruit and water to boil in saucepan. Cover; remove from heat. Let sit 30 minutes.

• Trim fat from tenderloins. Remove transparent membrane. Slice each tenderloin lengthwise, but don't cut right through. Cover each with wax paper. Flatten with back of knife or mallet until ½ inch/1 cm thick.

• Preheat oven to 325°F/160°C.

• Drain fruit, reserving liquid. Remove pits from prunes. Chop fruit. Combine with bread cubes, parsley, salt and lemon pepper in bowl. Place mixture on one flattened loin. Place other loin on top with narrow end of one over wide end of other. Tuck in ends. Wrap with bacon and secure with string or toothpicks. Set on rack in roasting pan. Roast 1¼ hours or until juices run clear when pierced.

• Boil reserved soaking liquid from fruit in small saucepan until reduced to ⅓ cup/75 mL.

• Remove pork from roasting pan. Keep warm. Drain excess fat from pan. Place pan over medium heat. Add vermouth, stirring and scraping up brown bits from bottom of pan with spoon. Add reduced liquid from fruit. Boil until slightly thickened.

• Slice pork. Arrange on serving platter. Spoon sauce on top.

Serves 4 to 6.

CHILI CON CARNE

I like my chili made with small chunks of beef. However, this recipe works equally well with ground beef—just omit the oil. Using dried kidney beans and simmering them slowly with the meat gives this nutritious, inexpensive dish an especially rich flavor.

2 cups	dried red kidney beans	500 mL
1 tbsp	vegetable oil	15 mL
1 lb	stewing beef (rump or chuck), cut into small cubes	500 g
1	medium onion, chopped	1
2	cloves garlic, finely chopped	2
1 tsp	hot red pepper flakes or to taste	5 mL
1 tsp	ground cumin	5 mL
1 tsp	chili powder	5 mL
1 tsp	dried oregano	5 mL
1	28-oz/796-mL can tomatoes, undrained	1
2 tbsp	tomato paste	25 mL
	Salt and freshly ground black pepper to taste	
	Grated cheese (Cheddar, mozzarella, Monterey Jack, etc.) for garnish	
	Sour cream or unflavored yogurt for garnish	

• Cover beans with cold water in bowl. Let soak 6 hours or overnight. (For less gaseous results, drain off water and repeat soaking process two to three times.)

• Heat oil in large heavy saucepan with lid. Add beef; brown over high heat. Don't overcrowd saucepan; do this in batches if necessary, returning all meat to pan when browned. Add onion and garlic. Cook over medium heat until softened, about 5 minutes. Add spices; cook 1 minute, stirring. Add tomatoes, tomato paste, beans and their soaking liquid. Bring to boil. Reduce heat; simmer, covered 2½ hours or until beans are tender, adding a little water if necessary. Add salt and pepper.

• Serve topped with grated cheese and a dollop of sour cream.

Serves 6 to 8.

NOTE: Leftover chili freezes like a dream. Leftovers make a fabulous meal of tacos served with tortillas, shredded lettuce, grated cheese, chopped tomatoes, chopped fresh coriander, unflavored yogurt and spicy taco sauce.

SATAYS WITH SPICY PEANUT SAUCE

What better barbecue fare than these super Southeast Asian-style satays with the best homemade peanut sauce I've tried. Use whatever meat you like as long as it's tender and good quality. Large shrimps work well, too. You'll probably have to visit Chinatown to find the shrimp paste, but it's well worth the effort. Or you can use its Indonesian equivalent, made by Conimex (called trassie oedang), which is available in many supermarkets.

1 lb	boneless skinless chicken breast, pork or beef tenderloin or lamb	500 g

MARINADE:

1 tbsp	ground coriander	15 mL
1	clove garlic, minced	1
1 tsp	ground cumin	5 mL
¼ tsp	turmeric	1 mL
2 tbsp	soy sauce	25 mL
2 tbsp	vegetable oil	25 mL
1 tbsp	lemon or lime juice	15 mL
2 tbsp	honey or corn syrup	25 mL

• Cut meat in bite-sized chunks or strips.
• Combine marinade ingredients in shallow non-metallic dish. Add meat. Toss to coat well. Let sit 2 hours at room temperature or overnight in fridge.

PEANUT SAUCE:

1	small onion, chopped	1
3	cloves garlic, peeled	3
1 tsp	Oriental shrimp paste	5 mL
1 tsp	Chinese chili sauce or to taste	5 mL
2 tsp	cumin seeds	10 mL
¼ tsp	turmeric	1 mL
¼ cup	fresh coriander leaves	50 mL
2 tbsp	vegetable oil	25 mL
1	14-oz/398-mL can coconut milk (about 1½ cups/375 mL)	1
1 tbsp	brown sugar	15 mL
	Juice of 1 lemon	
1 tsp	soy sauce or to taste	5 mL
½ cup	ground skinned unsalted peanuts	125 mL

- Blend onion, garlic, shrimp paste, chili sauce, cumin, turmeric and coriander leaves in food processor or blender until smooth.
- Heat oil in saucepan. Add blended mixture. Cook, stirring, 3 to 4 minutes or until aromatic. Add coconut milk. Bring to boil. Reduce heat; simmer about 5 minutes, stirring frequently. Add sugar, lemon juice, soy sauce and ground peanuts. Adjust soy sauce and chili sauce to taste. Cook until heated through. Makes about 2 cups/500 mL.
- Place meat chunks on wooden skewers that have been soaked in water for a few hours. Broil or grill on barbecue over medium heat until brown, crisp and cooked through. Serve with warmed peanut sauce on side for dipping.

Serves 4 to 6.

NOTE: You will have extra sauce. Store in fridge or freezer in airtight container.

CALVES' LIVER VENETIAN STYLE

I first tasted this divine dish when I visited Venice in the fall of 1986. The secret to cooking liver is to hardly cook it at all. Onions, on the other hand, taste best when slowly cooked to rich succulence. This Venetian specialty contains that magic formula and is guaranteed to convert almost anyone to liver!

3 tbsp	olive oil	45 mL
2	large onions, thinly sliced	2
1 lb	calves' liver, membrane removed and cut in strips ¼ inch/5 mm wide	500 g
	Salt and freshly ground black pepper to taste	
¼ cup	dry white wine	50 mL
1 tbsp	fresh lemon juice	15 mL
2 tbsp	chopped fresh parsley	25 mL

- Heat oil in large heavy skillet. Add onions. Saute over medium heat until golden, 8 to 10 minutes. Increase heat to medium-high. Push onions to side of pan; add a little more oil if skillet is dry. Add liver. Cook, stirring, about 2 minutes or until liver is just cooked. Add salt and pepper. Transfer mixture to warm serving dish or platter. Keep warm.
- Add wine and lemon juice to skillet. Bring to boil, stirring and scraping up brown bits from bottom of pan. Pour sauce over liver and onions on serving dish. Sprinkle with parsley. Serve with boiled new potatoes in their skins and a green salad.

Serves 4.

JAMBALAYA

"Cravin' Cajun" was the theme when this recipe for a Creole meal-in-a-pot appeared in the Sun. Yummy and easy to make, this makes a great dish for a party buffet. Serve it with cornbread (page 120), salad and some mint juleps to wash it all down.

1 tbsp	butter	15 mL
8 oz	smoked sausage (kielbasa), diced	250 g
8 oz	cooked ham, diced	250 g
2 tbsp	all-purpose flour	25 mL
1	medium onion, chopped	1
2	green onions, chopped	2
2	cloves garlic, finely chopped	2
¼ cup	chopped celery	50 mL
1	green pepper, cored, seeded and chopped	1
4	tomatoes, peeled, seeded and chopped (see page 10)	4
1	bay leaf	1
½ tsp	dried thyme	2 mL
¼ tsp	ground cumin	1 mL
½ tsp	dried oregano	2 mL
¼ tsp	cayenne pepper or to taste	1 mL
	Salt and freshly ground black pepper to taste	
3 cups	fish or chicken stock	750 mL
1 cup	long-grain rice	250 mL
12	shrimp, peeled and deveined	12
½ cup	cooked cubed chicken	125 mL

• Melt butter in large heavy saucepan over medium heat. Add sausage and ham. Saute until lightly browned. Sprinkle on flour. Cook, stirring, 1 minute. Add onions, garlic, celery and green pepper. Cook until softened, about 5 minutes. Stir in tomatoes, spices, stock and rice. Bring to boil. Reduce heat; simmer covered, 25 minutes or until rice is tender. Add shrimp and chicken. Cook, covered, 4 to 5 minutes or until shrimp are cooked and chicken is heated through.

Serves 4 to 6.

PEPPER-CRUSTED BEEF

A simply super barbecue recipe from one of Toronto's top food writers, Marg Fraser, who contributed it when she appeared as the Sun food section's Cook of the Week in 1985.

2 tbsp	Dijon mustard	25 mL
2 tbsp	black peppercorns, coarsely crushed with mallet or back of knife	25 mL
2 tsp	herbes de Provence or mixed herbs	10 mL
2 lb	beef (eye of round or tenderloin)	1 kg

• Blend together mustard, peppercorns and herbs in small bowl. Spread mixture over surface of beef, pressing peppercorns into meat. Spread leftover mixture on top of beef. (If desired, let beef sit at room temperature 1 hour at this point for maximum flavor.)

• Barbecue meat by indirect heat by centring it over drip pan placed between piles of hot coals in covered barbecue or firmly secured on spit. Cook until meat thermometer inserted in centre registers desired degree of doneness. Or roast in 400°F/200°C oven about 1 hour for rare beef.

Serves 6 to 8.

TOAD-IN-THE-HOLE

This creation brings back memories from my childhood days in London, England. The recipe appeared in a Mother's Day article I wrote in 1984 and comes from Pat MacKenzie, a mother of five who "still makes a double batch of it when the kids come to visit." Basically a Yorkshire pudding in which sausages play hide-and-seek, toad-in-the-hole makes a tasty supper served with beef gravy or favorite chutney and a big bowl of salad.

1⅓ cups	all-purpose flour	325 mL
1 tsp	salt	5 mL
	Freshly ground black pepper to taste	
3	eggs, lightly beaten	3
¾ cup	milk	175 mL
¾ cup	water	175 mL
1 lb	pork sausages	500 g

• Several hours before serving, prepare batter. Combine flour, salt and pepper in bowl. Add eggs, milk and water. Whisk together or beat with electric mixer until well blended. Let batter sit in fridge, whisking occasionally.

• Preheat oven to 400°F/200°C.

• Place sausages in 9 × 5-inch/2-L metal loaf pan. Bake in oven until browned on all sides, turning a few times, about 8 to 10 minutes. Drain off fat, leaving enough to cover bottom of pan. Pour batter over sausages in pan. Return to oven; bake 35 to 45 minutes or until top is brown and crisp.

Serves 4 to 6.

NOTE: Don't be upset if batter falls when toad-in-the-hole comes out of oven.

CREATE-YOUR-OWN STIR-FRY

Once you know the basic techniques and have some confidence, you can become a creative cook. This is especially true with the Oriental stir-fry—one of the most versatile, healthy, delicious ways to prepare food. Cut veggies on the diagonal for quicker cooking. I find it a good idea to blanch firm vegetables like broccoli florets and carrots by cooking them in boiling water for 1 to 2 minutes before adding them to the stir-fry. If using delicate vegetables like bean sprouts, add them at the last minute.

SAUCE:

1 cup	chicken stock or water	250 mL
1 tbsp	dark soy sauce or 2 tbsp (25 mL) light	15 mL
2 tbsp	dry sherry	25 mL
1 tbsp	cornstarch	15 mL
1 tsp	granulated sugar (optional)	5 mL

• Combine sauce ingredients in small bowl. Mix well. Set aside.

1 lb	meat, poultry or seafood (pork or beef tenderloin, chicken breast, shrimp, etc.)	500 g
¼ cup	vegetable oil	50 mL
2	cloves garlic, finely chopped	2
1 tbsp	finely chopped fresh ginger root	15 mL
2 cups	broccoli florets or other firm vegetables, cut in bite-sized pieces, approx.	500 mL
1 cup	sliced bok choy or other Chinese greens	250 mL
1 cup	snow peas, topped and tailed, or fresh peas	250 mL
3	green onions, chopped	3
¼ cup	toasted almonds, sesame seeds, cashews or other nuts (optional)	50 mL

• Cut meat into bite-sized chunks or slices 1 inch/2 cm long. If using shrimp, peel and devein.

• Heat oil in wok or large heavy skillet over high heat until very hot. Add garlic and ginger; stir-fry about 1 minute until softened but not brown. Add meat to wok. Stir-fry 2 to 5 minutes or until just cooked through. Transfer to plate with slotted spoon. Add broccoli to wok. Stir-fry 2 to 3 minutes or until tender-crisp. Add bok choy and snow peas. Stir-fry about 2 minutes or until tender-crisp.

• Return meat to wok. Push food up sides of wok. Stir sauce and pour into centre of wok. Cook, stirring, until sauce is thickened and all food in wok is coated. Stir in green onions. Garnish with toasted nuts if using. Serve at once with steamed rice or noodles.

Serves 4.

GRAVLAX WITH MUSTARD SAUCE

After a salmon fishing trip hosted by the B.C. Fisheries in the summer of '85, I returned home enthused about how wonderful that fish can taste. This recipe for gravlax—a Scandinavian way of marinating salmon that tastes a lot like the smoked version—is surprisingly easy to make and is a fabulous appetizer at parties. The mustard sauce is a must!

1	4-lb/2-kg fresh salmon, scaled, cleaned and cut in 2 fillets	1
1	bunch fresh dill, coarse stems removed	1

• Place one salmon fillet in large, shallow glass, porcelain or enamel dish. Place dill on top.

MARINADE:

¼ cup	coarse, kosher or sea salt	50 mL
¼ cup	granulated sugar	50 mL
2 tbsp	whole peppercorns (any color), crushed	25 mL
2 tbsp	vodka, gin or dry white wine	25 mL

• Combine marinade ingredients in bowl. Sprinkle over fish. Place second salmon fillet on top. Cover with foil. Place heavy weight (a brick or cans of food) on top. Let marinate in fridge 2 to 3 days, turning whole fish over every 12 hours and basting with juices.

• Remove salmon from marinade. Pat dry with paper towels. Place, skin-side up, on board. Slice as thinly as possible with sharp knife, wiggling knife to and fro as you slice.

MUSTARD SAUCE:

¼ cup	Dijon mustard	50 mL
1 tsp	dry mustard	5 mL
3 tbsp	granulated sugar	45 mL
2 tbsp	white or white wine vinegar	25 mL
¼ cup	peanut, safflower or sunflower oil	50 mL
¼ cup	finely chopped fresh dill	50 mL

• Combine mustards, sugar and vinegar in bowl. Add oil in thin stream, whisking constantly, until sauce thickens. (This can be done in food processor or blender.) Stir in dill. Serve on side with gravlax along with thinly sliced rye or pumpernickel bread.

Serves 14 to 16.

JONN'S TERRIFIC TUNA MELT

It's easy to get hooked on this delicious meal-on-a-bun from chef Jonn Richardson. The perfect weekend lunch with a green salad, a great breakfast for those willing to break with convention, and the ideal healthy meal for kids who don't like fish. Low-cal if you use water-packed tuna and skim milk cheese, this is one of my absolute favorites.

1	7-oz/199-mL can tuna, drained	1
2 tbsp	finely chopped onion	25 mL
2 tbsp	finely chopped green pepper	25 mL
2 tbsp	mayonnaise or unflavored low-fat yogurt	25 mL
½ tsp	Worcestershire sauce	2 mL
dash	Tabasco sauce	dash
	Salt and pepper to taste	
2	bagels, cut in half horizontally	2
8	slices tomato	8
4	slices onion	4
8	slices Swiss, Monterey Jack, mozzarella, Cheddar or other cheese	8

- Preheat oven to 350°F/180°C.
- Combine tuna, onion, green pepper, mayonnaise, Worcestershire, Tabasco, salt and pepper in bowl.
- Toast bagel halves. On each half, layer 2 tomato slices, 1 slice onion, one quarter of tuna mixture and 2 slices cheese. Bake in oven 4 to 5 minutes or until cheese melts.
- Place under broiler until cheese is brown and bubbly.

Serves 2 as main course.

CARLOTTA'S TUNA CASSEROLE

Carlotta Riggs of Oshawa won a case of Loblaws albacore solid white tuna and casserole dishes from Corning Ware for this classic recipe. This adaptation of her quick and easy concoction harks back to the fifties; it will likely bring a nostalgic tear to your eye, as it did to mine. Kids love it. It's good for you. It takes minutes to cook after a hard day at work. What more can I say?

1 cup	uncooked macaroni	250 mL
1	7-oz/199-mL can tuna, drained	1
1	small onion, finely chopped	1
1 cup	frozen or 10-oz/284-mL can peas, drained	250 mL
1	10-oz/284-mL can cream of chicken soup	1

½ cup	milk	125 mL
	Pepper to taste	
	Paprika for garnish	
½ cup	crushed potato chips	125 mL

- Preheat oven to 350°F/180°C.
- Cook macaroni in plenty of boiling salted water until al dente. Drain.
- Combine tuna, onion, peas, soup, milk and pepper in large bowl. Fold in cooked macaroni. Turn into lightly buttered 6-cup/1.5-L ovenproof dish. Sprinkle with paprika.
- Bake 20 minutes. Top with potato chips. Return to oven. Bake 10 minutes more.

Serves 4 with a salad and crusty bread.

MUSSELS MARINIÈRES

Debbie Harris, who appeared in "Room with a Stew" in the fall of '86—an article on how students can cook for themselves—claimed that this recipe was her weekend indulgence after a hard week of study at the University of Toronto. The elegant look and taste of this classic dish belie the fact that it is inexpensive and simple to make. Serve it with plenty of crusty French bread for dunking!

2 lb	unshelled mussels	1 kg
2 tbsp	butter or vegetable oil	25 mL
1	medium onion, chopped	1
½ cup	dry white wine	125 mL
½ cup	whipping cream (optional)	125 mL
	Salt and pepper to taste	
¼ cup	chopped fresh parsley	50 mL

- Scrub mussels well under cold running water, removing beards.
- Heat butter in large heavy saucepan with lid. Add onion; saute until softened, about 5 minutes. Do not brown. Add wine. Bring to boil. Add mussels. Return liquid to boil. Cover saucepan. Simmer mussels 4 to 5 minutes or until they open. Transfer mussels to warm serving bowl with slotted spoon, discarding any that have not opened. Keep mussels warm.
- Strain cooking liquid through cheesecloth or sieve lined with a J-cloth or paper towel. Return liquid to saucepan. Bring to boil. Reduce heat; simmer 2 minutes. Add cream, salt, pepper and parsley. Simmer 2 minutes or until slightly thickened. Pour over mussels.

Serves 2 hungry students as main course or 4 average humans as appetizer!

SALMONBURGERS

I got this recipe from the Food Media Conference in New York. What a great substitute for ground beef in a burger, especially if you believe all that stuff about Omega-3 fatty acids preventing heart disease. This version is sensational. Substitute two slightly beaten eggs for the mayonnaise if desired.

2	7-oz/199-mL cans salmon, drained (reserve liquid)	2
2 tsp	lemon juice	10 mL
2 tbsp	finely chopped fresh chives or green onion	25 mL
2 tbsp	finely chopped fresh parsley	25 mL
1 tbsp	finely chopped fresh dill (optional)	15 mL
1 tsp	dry mustard	5 mL
2 tbsp	freshly grated Parmesan cheese	25 mL
½ cup	breadcrumbs	125 mL
½ cup	mayonnaise	125 mL
	Freshly ground black pepper to taste	
	Vegetable oil for brushing	

- Preheat oven to 400°F/200°C.
- Lightly grease baking sheet.
- Combine all ingredients except oil in bowl. Mix well. Add small amount of reserved salmon liquid if necessary to moisten. Shape into 6 uniform patties. Place on prepared baking sheet. Bake 10 minutes. Brush tops of patties lightly with oil. Turn patties over. Bake 10 minutes more or until lightly browned. Serve on toasted buns with choice of garnishes (lettuce, tomato, pickles, etc.) as one would a hamburger.

Serves 6.

POULTRY

CHICKEN LEEK MOUSSE

In the summer of '84, I offered ideas for picnickers in an article called "Splendor on the Grass." This scrumptious chicken mousse from caterer Wendy Naismith is a fabulous pâté-style creation that's great on bread or eaten with a salad and some crusty bread.

½	sweet red pepper, cored, seeded and coarsely chopped	½
2	leeks, coarsely chopped	2
½ cup	butter	125 mL
¼ cup	chopped fresh parsley	50 mL
1 cup	fresh breadcrumbs	250 mL
1½ cups	light cream	375 mL
4	eggs, separated	4
3½ cups	cubed cooked chicken	875 mL
	Salt and pepper to taste	

- Preheat oven to 350°F/180°C.
- Lightly butter 6-cup/1.5-L mould or ovenproof dish.
- Process red pepper and leeks in food processor or blender until finely chopped.
- Melt butter in saucepan. Add pepper/leek mixture. Saute until softened, about 5 minutes. Add parsley. Remove from heat. Stir in breadcrumbs, ½ cup/125 mL cream and egg yolks. Transfer mixture to large bowl.
- Puree chicken in food processor with egg whites and remaining cream. Add salt and pepper.
- Fold chicken into vegetable mixture. Pour into prepared mould. Cover top with foil. Place in pan of hot water.
- Bake 45 minutes or until mixture sets. Cool. Chill.

Serves 10 to 12 as picnic dish.

BUFFALO CHICKEN WINGS

These originated at the Anchor Bar in Buffalo where the Bellissimo family have been making their secret version for many moons. This is a first-rate facsimile. The trick is to use Frank's Louisiana Hot Sauce made by Durkee, available at major supermarkets. Make the blue cheese dip—a mandatory accompaniment—at least an hour or two ahead so it has time to chill.

12	chicken wings, tips cut off (about 2 lb/1 kg)	12
	Peanut or vegetable oil for deep-frying	
¼ cup	butter	50 mL
¼ cup	Frank's Louisiana Hot Sauce or to taste	50 mL
1 tbsp	vinegar	15 mL

- Cut wings in half at joint if desired.
- Heat oil to 350°F/180°C or until piece of bread browns in 30 seconds. Fry wings in batches until crisp and brown, about 8 minutes. Drain on paper towels.
- Melt butter in small saucepan. Stir in hot sauce and vinegar. Place wings in large bowl. Pour sauce on top. Toss to coat wings. Transfer to serving platter. Serve with blue cheese dip (recipe below).

Serves 3 to 4 as appetizer.

BLUE CHEESE DIP:

1 cup	mayonnaise	250 mL
1	green onion, chopped	1
1	clove garlic, minced	1
¼ cup	finely chopped fresh parsley	50 mL
2 tbsp	lemon juice	25 mL
½ cup	unflavored yogurt or sour cream	125 mL
¼ cup	crumbled blue cheese	50 mL

- Combine dip ingredients in bowl. Mix well. Chill.

SUPER SOY ROAST CHICKEN

I learned this trick for roasting chicken from my mother. Soy sauce has the magnificent quality of browning and crisping chicken skin during roasting. It also adds enough flavor that you can even skip the orange juice and ginger root if desired. The perfect quick family meal.

3 tbsp	soy sauce	45 mL
	Freshly ground black pepper to taste	
1 tbsp	unsweetened orange juice	15 mL
1 tbsp	finely grated peeled fresh ginger root	15 mL
3 to 4 lb	roasting chicken	1.5 to 2 kg

- Preheat oven to 350°F/180°C.
- Combine soy sauce, pepper, juice and ginger root in small bowl.
- Place chicken in roasting pan. Brush liberally with soy sauce mixture. Bake 1 hour, basting at intervals with sauce, or until chicken is brown and crisp.

Serves 4 to 6.

LE SELECT'S COUSCOUS

This recipe from Le Select, one of Toronto's first and best bistro-style restaurants, appeared in the paper in response to a reader's request. A popular dish in Morocco and other North African countries, this dish is also a staple in many Parisian restaurants. Couscous is a delicate cracked wheat grain that can be found in health food and specialty stores or in some supermarkets.

4	chicken legs with thighs attached, halved at joint	4
	Salt and freshly ground black pepper to taste	
1 tbsp	vegetable oil	15 mL
4	sweet Italian sausages	4
2 tbsp	butter	25 mL
1	small onion, cut in bite-sized pieces	1
1	carrot, peeled and cut in bite-sized pieces	1
1	stalk celery, cut in bite-sized pieces	1
1	parsnip, peeled and cut in bite-sized pieces	1
¼	fresh fennel bulb, cut in bite-sized pieces	¼
½	each red and green pepper, cored, seeded and cut in bite-sized pieces	½
4 oz	fresh mushrooms, halved (about 1 cup/ 250 mL)	125 g
1	small unpeeled zucchini, cut in bite-sized pieces	1
	Salt and pepper to taste	
¼ tsp	ground coriander	1 mL
1	clove garlic, minced	1
¼ tsp	coriander seeds	1 mL
½ tsp	anise seeds	2 mL
1 tsp	tomato paste	5 mL
1 tsp	Tabasco sauce or to taste	5 mL
¼ cup	dry white wine	50 mL
2 cups	beef stock	500 mL
1 tbsp	softened butter	15 mL
1 tbsp	all-purpose flour	15 mL
2 cups	couscous	500 mL
1	fresh tomato, chopped	1
2	green onions, chopped	2

- Sprinkle chicken with salt and pepper. Heat oil in very large heavy saucepan. Add chicken and sausages. Cook over medium-high heat until browned all over. Remove from skillet. Cut sausages in chunks.
- Add butter to saucepan. Add onion, carrot, celery, parsnip and fennel. Saute about 5 minutes or until softened but not brown. Add peppers, mushrooms and zucchini. Saute 2 minutes more. Add salt, pepper and ground coriander. Transfer vegetables to plate. Drain excess fat from saucepan.
- Add garlic, coriander seeds, anise, tomato paste and Tabasco to saucepan. Cook over medium heat, stirring, 5 minutes. Add wine, stirring and scraping up brown bits from bottom of pan with spoon. Add stock. Bring to boil; reduce heat. Simmer 35 minutes.
- Combine softened butter with flour to form paste. Whisk into stock mixture, stirring constantly, until sauce boils. Strain through sieve. Return to skillet.
- Return chicken and sausage chunks to saucepan. Simmer, partially covered, about 40 minutes.
- Return vegetables to saucepan. Cook over medium heat until heated through.
- While chicken and sausages are cooking, prepare couscous according to package directions.
- To serve, place couscous on warmed serving dish or platter. Top with stew. Garnish with tomato and green onions.

Serves 6 to 8.

STICKY CHICKEN

This is one of those recipes that food snobs would sniff at—if they knew what they were eating, that is! This dish came to me via Lindsey Hermer-Bell, who in turn got it from a friend. A hit with kids of all ages and a cinch to make. Calorie counters can remove the chicken skin before cooking.

8	single boneless chicken breasts	8
1	250-mL bottle Russian salad dressing	1
2 tbsp	apricot jam	25 mL
1	pouch Lipton's onion soup mix	1

- Preheat oven to 350°F/180°C.
- Place chicken in greased ovenproof dish in a single layer.
- Blend remaining ingredients in bowl. Pour mixture over chicken. Bake 45 minutes or until chicken is tender.

Serves 6 to 8.

TANDOORI CHICKEN

This version of a classic Indian dish, in which chicken is marinated and then grilled in a clay oven, is probably my favorite recipe of all time. I've been making it for dinner parties and taking it cold on picnics for most of my adult life and have given the recipe to almost all my friends. Easy to make, it is stunning to look at, and loaded with spicy flavor. Serve with saffron rice (page 38), naan or chapatis for bread, and cucumber raita (page 42) as salad, and you've got a wonderful East Indian meal. And don't forget the mango chutney (page 181 or storebought) that's a must as a condiment. If using chicken parts, I like to buy breasts and legs only for this dish and cut them into serving-sized pieces. You can also marinate, roast and even serve the chicken in one piece.

3 to 4 lb	chicken parts or 1 whole chicken	1.5 to 2 kg
2 tsp	coriander seeds	10 mL
1 tsp	cumin seeds	5 mL
1 cup	unflavored yogurt	250 mL
2	cloves garlic, chopped	2
1 tbsp	chopped fresh ginger root	15 mL
1 tsp	salt	5 mL
	Juice of 1 lemon (about ¼ cup/50 mL)	
½ tsp	hot red pepper flakes or to taste	2 mL
½ tsp	ground turmeric	2 mL
	Lime and tomato wedges for garnish	
	Sprigs of fresh coriander or parsley for garnish	

• Prick holes in chicken skin. Place in large shallow dish in single layer.

• Toast coriander and cumin seeds in heavy skillet over low heat, shaking constantly, 2 to 3 minutes or until aromatic. Grind in blender or food processor until powdery. Add remaining ingredients except garnishes. Blend until smooth. Pour mixture over chicken. Let marinate, covered, a few hours at room temperature or overnight in fridge.

• Preheat oven to 350°F/180°C.

• Place chicken pieces in single layer in large ovenproof dish (I find ceramic or clay work best), making sure pieces are coated with marinade.

• Bake 1 hour or until crisp and brown. Serve on bed of lettuce garnished with lime and tomato wedges and fresh coriander sprigs.

Serves 4 to 6.

African Chicken with Pine Nuts

The crunch of pine nuts, the aroma of allspice and cinnamon, and chunks of juicy chicken make this a marvellous one-dish meal that is perfect make-ahead fare. From the Doha (North African) pavilion at the 1984 Caravan—Toronto's multicultural festival.

3 to 4 lb	roasting chicken	1.5 to 2 kg
	Salt and pepper to taste	
½ cup	pine nuts	125 mL
½ cup	slivered almonds	125 mL
1 tbsp	butter	15 mL
1	medium onion, finely chopped	1
8 oz	ground beef or lamb	250 g
1 cup	long-grain rice	250 mL
1 tsp	ground allspice	5 mL
¼ tsp	ground cinnamon	1 mL
	Salt and pepper to taste	
	Chopped fresh parsley for garnish	
	(optional)	

• Place chicken in large heavy saucepan with lid. Add enough water to cover. Add salt and pepper. Bring to boil. Skim off scum from surface. Cover; simmer about 45 minutes or until chicken is tender. Remove chicken, reserving 2 cups/500 mL cooking liquid.

• Cool chicken enough to handle. Remove meat from bones; discard skin and bones. Cut meat into bite-sized pieces.

• Preheat oven to 350°F/180°C.

• Lightly butter large dish or mould.

• Shaking constantly, toast pine nuts in heavy skillet over low heat until golden brown, about 5 minutes. Repeat with almonds. Set nuts aside in separate small bowls.

• Heat butter in large saucepan with lid. Saute onion until softened, about 5 minutes. Add ground meat; cook until browned. Add rice and pine nuts, stirring constantly. Cook 2 minutes. Add reserved cooking liquid, allspice, cinnamon, salt and pepper. Bring to boil. Cover; reduce heat. Simmer until liquid is absorbed, 20 to 30 minutes.

• Arrange chicken pieces on bottom of prepared dish. Top with rice mixture. Press down with back of spoon.

• Bake 30 minutes. Invert onto warm serving platter. Sprinkle with toasted almonds and chopped parsley if using. Serve with a green salad and plain yogurt flavored with chopped fresh mint.

Serves 4 to 6.

CHICKEN BREASTS PEACHES'N'CREAM

A rich, creamy chicken concoction from magazine editor Liz Primeau, who was Cook of the Week in the Sun food section in January, 1985. Primeau, who has enjoyed cooking since she was a teenager, makes this dish for her family when they visit on weekends. This is best made with fresh peaches in season.

¼ cup	all-purpose flour	50 mL
	Salt and pepper to taste	
½ tsp	dried thyme	2 mL
6	single chicken breasts, skinned and boned	6
2 tbsp	butter	25 mL
2 tbsp	peach brandy (optional)	25 mL
1	small onion, chopped	1
1 cup	chicken stock	250 mL
1 cup	whipping cream	250 mL
1 cup	sliced fresh peaches	250 mL

• Combine flour, salt, pepper and thyme in shallow dish. Dredge chicken in flour mixture; shake off excess.

• Heat butter in large skillet. Add chicken; saute until browned on all sides, 5 to 7 minutes per side. Do not overcook. (It will cook more in cream later.)

• Heat brandy if using. Remove chicken from heat and pour brandy over chicken; ignite. When flames die down, transfer chicken to warmed platter. Keep warm.

• Add onion to skillet in which chicken was cooked. Saute 3 minutes. Do not brown. Add stock. Bring to boil. Boil until reduced by half, stirring up brown bits from bottom of pan. Strain off liquid, pressing down on onion before discarding. Return liquid to skillet. Whisk in cream. Simmer until cream thickens slightly. Add peaches and chicken to skillet. Cook until heated through, 3 to 5 minutes.

• Arrange chicken on warmed platter. Pour sauce on top.

Serves 4 to 6.

CRUNCHY CHICKEN CASSEROLE

An all-Canadian standby, the origins of which have become hazy over the years. Fabulous at potluck meals and a great dish to whip up for brunch or bridge. This was one idea I gave in an article called "Feeding the Pack"—ideas for transportable food the whole cub or brownie pack will love. Usually made with chicken, this is also a great way to use up leftover turkey.

¼ cup	butter	50 mL
3 cups	sliced celery	750 mL
1	small onion, diced	1
	Salt and pepper to taste	
¼ cup	all-purpose flour	50 mL
1¾ cups	milk	425 mL
2 cups	diced cooked chicken or turkey	500 mL
1 cup	grated Cheddar cheese	250 mL

- Preheat oven to 400°F/200°C.
- Lightly butter large ovenproof dish.
- Heat butter in large saucepan. Add celery; saute 5 minutes. Add onions, salt and pepper; saute 3 minutes or until softened. Sprinkle on flour. Stir to combine. Slowly add milk, stirring constantly. Cook, stirring, until mixture comes to boil and thickens. Stir in chicken and cheese. Turn into prepared dish.

TOPPING:

½ cup	sliced almonds	125 mL
½ cup	all-purpose flour	125 mL
	Salt and pepper to taste	
¼ cup	cold butter	50 mL
½ cup	grated Cheddar cheese	125 mL

- Shaking constantly, toast almonds in heavy skillet over low heat until golden brown, about 5 minutes.
- Combine flour, salt and pepper in bowl. Cut in butter with two knives or pastry cutter until mixture resembles coarse crumbs. Stir in cheese and almonds. Sprinkle on chicken mixture.
- Bake 30 to 40 minutes or until golden brown.

Serves 4 to 6.

NOTE: Can be assembled ahead of time and baked as needed.

BARBECUED CHICKEN BURGERS

A standby at my house during barbecue season. Lower in fat than burgers made with ground beef, these rate even higher for juicy taste and texture. Serve like regular burgers with lettuce, tomato and other usual garnishes. You can vary this theme by skipping the marinade altogether and basting the chicken breasts with your favorite barbecue sauce. I like to use polyunsaturated oil such as soybean, safflower, sunflower or corn.

MARINADE:

½ cup	sunflower, safflower or corn oil	125 mL
2 tbsp	light soy sauce	25 mL
3 tbsp	red wine vinegar or lemon juice	45 mL
1 tsp	minced peeled fresh ginger root (optional)	5 mL
1	clove garlic, minced	1
	Freshly ground pepper to taste	

• Combine ingredients in shallow non-metallic dish large enough to hold chicken breasts in single layer.

4	single boneless chicken breasts	4

• Place chicken breasts in dish with marinade. Turn to coat well. Let marinate at least 1 hour at room temperature or overnight in fridge.
• Remove breasts from marinade, reserving marinade for basting. Barbecue over medium heat about 5 minutes per side or until cooked through, basting with reserved marinade at intervals. Serve with toasted buns and burger garnishes.

Serves 4.

CHICKEN MIGUEL

Another recipe from chef Jonn Richardson, who got the inspiration for this Mexican-flavored dish while working at Carlyle restaurant in Yorkville. Jalapeño peppers and goat's cheese combine to make a zesty filling for the juicy, nut-encrusted chicken.

FILLING:

4 oz	goat's cheese (room temperature)	125 g
1 tsp	finely chopped and seeded jalapeño peppers (canned or fresh), or to taste	5 mL
1 tsp	finely chopped fresh coriander	5 mL
	Salt and pepper to taste	

- Combine filling ingredients in bowl. For best flavor, leave overnight in fridge and bring to room temperature before using.

ORANGE BUTTER:

1 tsp	grated orange peel	5 mL
½ tsp	orange liqueur (optional)	2 mL
½ tsp	finely chopped seeded jalapeño peppers	2 mL
¼ cup	butter (room temperature)	50 mL

- Combine orange butter ingredients in bowl. Place on sheet of plastic wrap. Shape into tube about 1 inch/2 cm in diameter. Wrap in plastic wrap. Chill. (The butter can be made ahead.)

4	single chicken breasts, skinned and boned	4
½ cup	all-purpose flour	125 mL
2	eggs, beaten	2
1 cup	finely ground hazelnuts	250 mL
¼ cup	breadcrumbs	50 mL
	Salt and pepper to taste	
¼ cup	vegetable oil	50 mL

- Preheat oven to 375°F/190°C.
- Make incision along side of each breast to form pocket. Fill with equal amounts of filling.
- Place three bowls on counter. Fill one with flour, one with beaten egg and the third with hazelnuts, breadcrumbs, salt and pepper mixed together.
- Dredge each breast in flour, then dip in egg and coat well with hazelnut mixture.
- Heat oil in large skillet. Saute breasts over medium heat until lightly browned on both sides, about 2 minutes per side, taking care not to burn. Place on baking sheet. Bake in oven 15 minutes or until cooked through. Transfer to warmed platter.
- Cut orange butter into ¼-inch/5-mm slices. Place two slices on each chicken breast.

Serves 4.

NOTE: Saute accompanying vegetables in remaining orange butter if desired.

CHICKEN OR FISH-IN-A-POUCH

This contemporary version of the classic French method of cooking "en papillotte" makes one of the tastiest low-cal meals going. The foil pouch that replaces the classic parchment paper envelope works well for chicken breasts or fish fillets. This is the perfect meal for a single person who doesn't want to slave over a hot stove. The aroma that greets you when you open the pouch at the table is reason enough to try it. The pouches can be frozen and then re-heated still frozen or thawed. This recipe is for one person but can be multiplied to serve several.

1 tsp	softened butter or oil	5 mL
1	4-oz/125-g chicken breast, skinned and boned or fillet of firm-fleshed fish (cod, halibut, salmon, trout, etc.)	1
2 tbsp	finely chopped onions, shallots, celery or mushrooms	25 mL
1 tsp	finely chopped fresh herbs (dill, parsley, tarragon, etc.) or peeled fresh ginger root	5 mL
2 to 3 tbsp	chicken or fish stock or dry white wine	25 to 45 mL

- Preheat oven to 400°F/200°C.
- Cut foil in square or circle large enough to hold chicken or fish. Brush butter or oil over surface of foil. Place chicken or fish, onions and herbs in centre. Pull up sides of foil. Pour in stock or wine. Form into pouch and crimp edges of foil to seal.
- Place on baking sheet. Bake 20 to 25 minutes for chicken, 10 minutes per inch of thickness for fish. Serve unwrapped pouch on plate with accompanying vegetables; open at table.

Serves 1.

NOTE: For a whole meal-in-a-pouch, place vegetables of choice (snow peas, broccoli florets, sliced carrots, etc.) in pouch to cook with chicken or fish.

WOLFGANG PUCK'S GARLIC GRILLED CHICKEN

Movie stars and foodies gather at Wolfgang Puck's two L.A. eateries, Spago and Chinois, to enjoy the innovative cuisine of this creative young chef. Puck gave me this recipe when he was visiting chef at the Sutton Place hotel in the fall of '85. His way of barbecuing chicken is one of the simplest and most delicious that I've tried.

1	bulb garlic, separated into cloves and peeled	1
¼ cup	chopped Italian parsley	50 mL
	Salt and freshly ground black pepper to taste	
4	large single chicken breasts, bone in	4
	Vegetable oil or melted butter for brushing	
2 tbsp	butter	25 mL
	Juice of 1 lemon	

- Preheat barbecue or broiler to medium hot.
- Bring small pot of water to boil. Add garlic cloves and boil 1 minute; drain. Cut in paper-thin slices. Toss in small bowl with parsley and a little salt and pepper.
- Stuff about 1 tsp/5 mL garlic mixture between skin and flesh of each chicken breast. Reserve remaining mixture.
- Grill chicken over medium hot coals, brushing at intervals with oil, 7 to 10 minutes per side or until just cooked through. Do not overcook.
- Heat butter in small saucepan. Add remaining garlic mixture. Saute a few minutes or until garlic is soft. Add lemon juice and salt and pepper to taste.
- Serve chicken drizzled with sauce, accompanied by stir-fried vegetables, crusty bread, salad, etc.

Serves 4.

BARBECUED CHICKEN WINGS

Thomas Williams, a color technician at the Sun, contributed these super barbecued wings to a 1986 article I wrote on Father's Day called "Father Cooks Best." These spicy wings that can be barbecued or broiled are a big hit with Williams' son, Joel—as I'm sure they'll be with you.

12	chicken wings, tips cut off (about 2 lb/1 kg)	12
1 cup	ketchup	250 mL
½ cup	water	125 mL
2 tbsp	Dijon mustard	25 mL
3 tbsp	white or malt vinegar	45 mL
1 tbsp	brown sugar	15 mL
2 tbsp	Worcestershire sauce	25 mL
1	clove garlic, minced	1
1 tsp	lemon juice	5 mL
1 tsp	hot pepper sauce or to taste	5 mL
	Salt to taste	

- Cut wings in half at joint.
- Combine remaining ingredients in non-metallic bowl. Add wings. Toss to coat. Marinate 1 to 2 hours at room temperature or overnight in fridge.
- Broil or grill wings 10 to 15 minutes per side. Serve with Mexican salsa (available bottled in major supermarkets) or with dipping sauce of choice.

Serves 3 to 4.

EASY CURRIED CHICKEN

Food stylist, cookbook author and food writer Kate Bush is also a mother of two. Her favorite family meals are easy and loaded with taste. This dish fits that bill with bells on!

MARINADE:

2 tbsp	curry powder	25 mL
1 tbsp	paprika	15 mL
1 tsp	Worcestershire sauce	5 mL
dash	Tabasco or other hot sauce	dash
	Juice of 2 lemons (about ½ cup/125 mL)	
	Freshly ground pepper to taste	

- Combine marinade ingredients in large non-metallic bowl or dish.

1	medium chicken, cut in serving pieces	1
1 tbsp	vegetable oil	15 mL
2 tbsp	brown sugar	25 mL
2	medium onions, sliced	2
1	14-oz/398-mL can tomatoes, drained and chopped	1
2 tbsp	all-purpose flour	25 mL

• Pat chicken dry with paper towel. Toss chicken in marinade to coat well. There may seem to be little marinade for this but don't worry, it's enough. Cover. Refrigerate overnight or at least 2 hours at room temperature.

• Heat oil in large skillet. Add brown sugar. Stir to combine. Add chicken, a few pieces at a time. Brown on all sides over medium heat, being careful that sugar doesn't burn. Transfer chicken to large saucepan or casserole with lid. Add remaining marinade, onions and tomatoes. Simmer, covered, 30 to 40 minutes or until chicken is tender. Transfer chicken to warm serving dish.

• Place flour in small bowl. Add a little of hot cooking liquid. Whisk to form smooth paste. Return mixture to saucepan. Simmer, whisking constantly, until sauce thickens slightly, 2 to 3 minutes. Pour over chicken. Serve with pappadums, East Indian bread, Indonesian shrimp chips and a variety of condiments such as sliced cucumber or apples, chutney, peanuts and mandarin oranges.

Serves 4.

HONEY-GLAZED ROAST CHICKEN

Honey gives extra crispness and a hint of sweetness to this terrific, simple dish that once again proves the cooking maxim: Less is more.

½ cup	liquid honey	125 mL
¼ cup	soy sauce	50 mL
2	cloves garlic, minced	2
2 tbsp	butter	25 mL
3 to 4 lb	roasting chicken	1.5 to 2 kg

• Preheat oven to 350°F/180°C.

• Combine honey, soy sauce, garlic and butter in small saucepan. Bring to boil. Reduce heat; simmer 5 minutes.

• Place chicken in roasting pan. Bake 15 minutes. Brush liberally with sauce. Bake 45 minutes more, basting with remaining sauce at intervals, or until chicken is cooked through.

Serves 4 to 6.

CHICKEN LIVERS TORONTO

Jacques Pépin, French chef, cookbook author and TV personality, was visiting the Bonnie Stern School of Cooking in the fall of '85. He created this dish for the Sun food section when I surprised him with a whole chicken plus a pound of chicken livers and challenged him to come up with instant recipes. The dauntless Pépin didn't chicken out. In fact, this recipe is one of the best ways I've found to cook chicken livers—a much underrated delicacy.

1 lb	chicken livers	500 g
2 tbsp	butter	25 mL
1 tbsp	vegetable or peanut oil	15 mL
½ cup	thinly sliced leeks or green onions	125 mL
¼ cup	red wine vinegar	50 mL
3	cloves garlic, minced	3
½ cup	chicken stock or water	125 mL
1	large ripe tomato, seeded and chopped	1
	Salt and pepper to taste	
dash	Tabasco sauce	dash
2 tbsp	chopped chives or green onions	25 mL

• Clean livers, removing fat and green sac. (The green sac causes a bitter taste).

• Heat butter and oil in large heavy skillet over high heat. Saute livers 1 minute, stirring constantly. Livers should not overlap. Cook in two batches if necessary. With slotted spoon, place livers in sieve set over bowl to catch juices.

• Add leeks to skillet in which livers were cooked. Saute over medium-high heat until softened, about 5 minutes. Add vinegar and garlic. Cook until vinegar has almost evaporated and mixture is syrupy, about 3 minutes. Add stock, tomato and juices drained from livers. Bring to boil. Reduce heat to simmer. Add salt, pepper, Tabasco and livers. Warm gently without boiling. Sprinkle with chives. Serve with new boiled potatoes or rice and steamed veggies.

Serves 4.

CHICKEN CASHEW STIR-FRY

"Let's Create a Stir-Fry" was the challenge for four Toronto cooks in an article I wrote in November, 1985. One of the healthiest, tastiest and easiest of meals to prepare, the stir-fry has deservedly come into its own in a big way. This one came from Toronto's Rivoli restaurant and uses chicken and cashews. Substitute shrimp for chicken, use almonds instead of cashews and vary the ingredients as your mood and the contents of your fridge dictate. For guidelines on inventing a stir-fry, see page 92.

	SAUCE:	
3 tbsp	oyster sauce	45 mL
⅓ cup	dry sherry	75 mL
	Freshly ground black pepper to taste	

• Combine sauce ingredients in small bowl. Set aside.

¼ cup	vegetable oil	50 mL
3	single chicken breasts, boned, skinned and cut in chunks	3
3	cloves garlic, finely chopped	3
1	medium onion, cut in chunks (about 1 cup/ 250 mL)	1
1 cup	unsalted roasted cashews, a few reserved for garnish	250 mL
1	sweet red pepper, cored, seeded and cut in strips	1
½ cup	chopped celery	125 mL
8 oz	snow peas, topped and tailed (about 2 cups/ 500 mL)	250 g
1 cup	canned Chinese straw mushrooms, drained	250 mL

• Heat oil in wok or large heavy skillet until very hot. Add chicken, garlic and onion. Reduce heat to medium-high. Stir-fry 3 to 4 minutes or until chicken is almost cooked through. Add cashews and remaining vegetables. Stir-fry 2 to 3 minutes more or until vegetables are tender-crisp. Add sauce. Toss and cook about 1 minute or until food is coated. Sprinkle with reserved cashews. Serve at once over steamed rice or noodles.

Serves 4.

FIVE-SPICE CHICKEN WINGS

The Chinese five-spice mixture, available in most Chinese groceries, is the key ingredient to these wings from actress Michelle Scarabelli, who got the idea from a Vietnamese chef. Baked in the oven, they have the advantage of being lower in fat than their deep-fried counterparts.

MARINADE:

⅓ cup	vegetable oil	75 mL
1 tbsp	lemon juice	15 mL
2 tbsp	Worcestershire sauce	25 mL
1 tbsp	red wine vinegar	15 mL
⅓ cup	soy sauce	75 mL
1 tbsp	Dijon mustard	15 mL
dash	Tabasco sauce or to taste	dash
2 tbsp	honey or molasses	25 mL
pinch	ground black pepper	pinch
1 tsp	Chinese five-spice powder	5 mL

• Combine marinade ingredients in large plastic bowl with tight-fitting lid.

16	chicken wings, tips cut off	16
½ cup	sesame seeds	125 mL

• Cut wings in half at joint if desired. Place in marinade. Put lid on tightly. Shake to coat well. Let marinate in fridge at least 2 hours, preferably overnight.
• Preheat oven to 350°F/180°C.
• Remove wings from marinade, reserving marinade for basting. Place sesame seeds in shallow dish. Add wings; roll to coat well.
• Line baking sheet with foil. Place wings on foil. Bake 45 minutes, basting occasionally with reserved marinade. Brown under broiler 2 to 3 minutes or until crisp.

Serves 4 as appetizer.

BREADS, MUFFINS, COOKIES AND SQUARES

DOUBLE CORN CHEDDAR MUFFINS

We came up with this fabulous muffin for the article "Breakfast of Champions" in January, 1987. It's becoming increasingly clear that the maxim about eating breakfast "like a king/queen" makes darned good nutritional sense. These muffins combine the protein of cheese and the fibre of cornmeal with super taste. They are best served piping hot from the oven and also make the ideal mate for a bowl of steaming hot chili or hearty soup.

1 cup	yellow cornmeal	250 mL
1 cup	all-purpose flour	250 mL
1 tbsp	baking powder	15 mL
½ tsp	baking soda	2 mL
½ tsp	salt	2 mL
2 tbsp	granulated sugar	25 mL
2	eggs, slightly beaten	2
1¼ cups	buttermilk	300 mL
¼ cup	vegetable oil	50 mL
1 cup	frozen and thawed or canned and drained corn kernels	250 mL
1	fresh or canned jalapeño pepper, seeded and finely chopped (optional)	1
1 cup	grated old Cheddar cheese	250 mL

- Preheat oven to 400°F/200°C
- Lightly grease muffin tin.
- Combine cornmeal, flour, baking powder, baking soda, salt and sugar in bowl. Mix well.
- Combine eggs, buttermilk, oil, corn, jalapeño and ½ cup/125 mL cheese in large bowl. Mix well.
- Stir flour mixture into egg mixture just until moistened. Do not over-mix. Spoon into prepared muffin tin. Sprinkle tops of muffins with remaining cheese. Bake 20 to 25 minutes or until golden and firm to touch in centre.

Makes 1 dozen medium muffins.

OATMEAL RAISIN MUFFINS

Sun reader Judy Downey of Oshawa sent us this recipe for a delicious moist muffin with the fibre and flavor of oatmeal. Use whatever dried fruit or nuts you fancy—raisins, apricots, prunes, dates or pecans.

1 cup	milk (room temperature)	250 mL
1 tbsp	white vinegar	15 mL
1 cup	quick-cooking (not instant) rolled oats	250 mL
1 cup	all-purpose flour	250 mL
1 tsp	baking powder	5 mL
½ tsp	baking soda	2 mL
½ tsp	salt	2 mL
¼ tsp	ground ginger	1 mL
1 cup	brown sugar	250 mL
1	egg, lightly beaten	1
½ cup	vegetable oil	125 mL
1 tbsp	molasses	15 mL
1½ cups	dried fruit or nuts	375 mL

• Combine milk and vinegar in large bowl. Let sit 10 minutes. Stir in oats. Let sit 1 hour.

• Preheat oven to 375°F/190°C.

• Lightly butter muffin tins or line with paper baking cups.

• Combine flour, baking powder, baking soda, salt, ginger and brown sugar in medium bowl.

• Beat egg, oil and molasses in separate bowl. Stir into oatmeal mixture. Add flour mixture and dried fruit or nuts. Mix just until combined. Don't overmix. Spoon into muffin tins. Bake 20 to 25 minutes or until toothpick inserted comes out clean.

Makes about 1 dozen large muffins.

REFRIGERATOR BRAN MUFFINS

This is unequivocally the best homemade bran muffin I have eaten. Whip up this big batch of batter and bake them at breakfast as required. Ready when you are, these muffins are fairly low in fat and loaded with fibre. Eat them with a piece of cheese or low-fat yogurt topped with fruit, and you've got a breakfast bursting with nutrients. We adapted a recipe from reader Gloria Costenuck of Mississauga to come up with this winner.

2½ cups	granulated sugar	625 mL
4	eggs	4
1 cup	vegetable oil	250 mL
1 tbsp	salt	15 mL
8 tsp	baking soda	40 mL
5½ cups	all-purpose flour	1.375 L
4 cups	buttermilk	1 L
2 cups	All-Bran or other bran bud cereal	500 mL
3 cups	bran flakes	750 mL
2 cups	raisins	500 mL

• Beat sugar, eggs, oil and salt in very large bowl or plastic pail until thick and creamy.

• Sift baking soda and flour into separate bowl.

• Add half each of buttermilk, flour mixture, cereals and raisins to sugar/egg mixture in pail. Stir to combine. Add remaining halves of ingredients. Stir until just combined. Don't overmix.

• Refrigerate two days before baking or at least overnight.

• Preheat oven to 375°F/190°C.

• Lightly butter muffin tins or line with paper baking cups. Spoon in batter. Bake 20 to 25 minutes or until toothpick inserted comes out clean.

Makes about 4 dozen large muffins.

NOTE: Batter will keep in fridge at least 1 month, tightly covered.

ZUCCHINI BREAD

Here's one way to use up all those home-grown zucchini. This recipe comes from Ruth Fremes, host of CFTO's national cooking show, "What's Cooking with Ruth Fremes." The chocolate chips were my idea. This recipe makes two loaves; eat one now and freeze the other.

¼ cup	chopped walnuts	50 mL
⅓ cup	slivered almonds	75 mL
2¾ cups	all-purpose flour	675 mL
½ cup	wholewheat flour	125 mL
2 tsp	ground cinnamon	10 mL
1 tsp	ground nutmeg	5 mL
2 tsp	baking soda	10 mL
1 tsp	baking powder	5 mL
1 tsp	salt	5 mL
½ cup	shredded coconut	125 mL
⅓ cup	raisins	75 mL
2½ cups	(2 to 3 medium) zucchini, unpeeled and grated	625 mL
½ cup	semisweet chocolate chips (optional)	125 mL
	Grated rind of 1 lemon	
4	eggs	4
1½ cups	granulated sugar	375 mL
¾ cup	vegetable oil	175 mL

- Preheat oven to 350°F/180°C.
- Lightly butter two 9 × 5-inch/2-L loaf pans.
- Shaking constantly, toast walnuts and almonds in heavy skillet over low heat until golden brown, about 5 minutes. Cool.
- Combine flours, cinnamon, nutmeg, baking soda, baking powder and salt in large bowl. Add walnuts, almonds, coconut, raisins, grated zucchini, chocolate chips and lemon peel. Toss to coat well.
- Beat eggs until foamy in separate bowl. Add sugar and oil. Beat until thick and creamy.
- Gradually stir liquid ingredients into flour mixture until combined. Don't overmix.
- Divide batter between prepared pans. Bake 1 hour or until toothpick inserted comes out clean. Cool 10 minutes in pan. Turn onto wire racks.

GLAZE:

¼ cup	granulated sugar	50 mL
2 tbsp	lemon juice	25 mL

- Combine sugar and lemon juice in small bowl. Drizzle over warm cakes.

CORNBREAD

Great with a bowl of steaming chili, terrific with Cajun food such as jambalaya, and divine on its own with a piece of cheese. The cornbread is also a key ingredient in our cornbread stuffing (page 186), to dress up that festive bird.

1½ cups	yellow cornmeal	375 mL
1 cup	sifted all-purpose flour	250 mL
¼ cup	granulated sugar	50 mL
1 tbsp	baking powder	15 mL
1 tsp	salt	5 mL
1½ cups	milk	375 mL
¾ cup	melted butter, cooled	175 mL
2	eggs, lightly beaten	2

- Preheat oven to 400°F/200°C.
- Lightly butter 8-inch/2-L square baking pan.
- Combine cornmeal, flour, sugar, baking powder and salt in large bowl.
- Combine milk, butter and eggs in separate bowl. Stir into cornmeal mixture just until moistened. Do not overmix. Turn batter into prepared pan. Bake 25 minutes or until golden.

NOTE: If using in cornbread stuffing, make one day ahead.

AMAZING BANANA BREAD

Frances Beaulieu, artist, gourmet cook and author/designer of Sun *recipe cartoon, Recipix, put together all her favorite ingredients to come up with this unbeatable quickbread. Now there's no excuse for throwing away those blackened, overripe bananas that sit languishing in the fruit bowl!*

½ cup	vegetable oil	125 mL
2	large ripe bananas, mashed	2
1 cup	granulated sugar	250 mL
2	eggs	2
1 tsp	vanilla	5 mL
1¼ cups	all-purpose flour	300 mL
1 tsp	baking soda	5 mL
½ tsp	ground cinnamon	2 mL
¼ tsp	ground nutmeg	1 mL
½ cup	chopped walnuts	125 mL
½ cup	semisweet chocolate chips	125 mL
½ cup	shredded coconut	125 mL

- Preheat oven to 350°F/180°C.
- Lightly butter 9 × 5-inch/2-L loaf pan.
- Beat together oil, bananas, sugar, eggs and vanilla in bowl.
- Sift flour, baking soda, cinnamon and nutmeg into separate bowl. Stir into banana mixture. Stir in walnuts, chocolate chips and coconut. Pour into prepared pan.
- Bake 1 hour or until toothpick inserted comes out clean.

BEAUTIFUL BEER BREAD

You'll wonder why you ever bothered with yeast when you try this magnificent bread recipe from the folks at Labatt's. The perfect mate for soup or chili and a crisp green salad, this is a cinch to make.

1	355-mL bottle beer (about 1½ cups)	1
1 tbsp	sesame seeds	15 mL
2¾ cups	all-purpose flour	675 mL
4 tsp	baking powder	20 mL
1 tbsp	granulated sugar	15 mL
½ tsp	salt	2 mL
¼ tsp	dry mustard	1 mL
1¼ cups	grated old Cheddar cheese	300 mL

- Preheat oven to 350°F/180°C.
- Lightly grease 8 × 4-inch/1.5-L loaf pan.
- Uncap beer; let sit until at room temperature.
- Shaking constantly, toast sesame seeds in heavy skillet over low heat until golden brown, about 5 minutes.
- Combine flour, baking powder, sugar, salt and mustard in large bowl. Mix well. Add 1 cup/250 mL cheese; mix well. Pour in beer. Stir just to combine. Pour batter into prepared pan. Sprinkle top with remaining shredded cheese and toasted sesame seeds.
- Bake 45 to 50 minutes or until toothpick comes out clean. Cool a few minutes before turning out onto wire rack. Best served warm.

SAN FRAN CHOCOLATE FOGGY BARS

In 1986, these bars won Chocolatier *magazine's COCO Award. The recipe came from Barbara Feldman of San Francisco, California. These bars are so rich and soft that you might think you've undercooked them, but they will firm up to melt-in-the-mouth perfection after a brief time in the fridge. Use only top-quality chocolate, and eat these one at a time!*

1 lb	bittersweet chocolate, finely chopped	500 g
1 cup	unsalted butter, cut in chunks	250 mL
⅓ cup	strong coffee	75 mL
4	eggs	4
1½ cups	granulated sugar	375 mL
½ cup	all-purpose flour	125 mL
2 cups	walnut halves, coarsely chopped	500 mL

• Preheat oven to 375°F/190°C.

• Line 13 × 9-inch/3.5-L baking pan with double thickness of aluminium foil so that foil extends 2 inches/5 cm beyond sides of pan. Lightly butter bottom and sides of foil.

• Heat chocolate, butter and coffee in top of double boiler over barely simmering water, stirring frequently until melted and smooth. Remove pan from heat. Cool 10 minutes, stirring occasionally.

• Beat eggs until foamy in large bowl, using electric mixer on high speed. Gradually add sugar. Continue to beat 2 minutes or until mixture is light and fluffy. Reduce mixer speed to low; gradually beat in chocolate mixture until just blended. Stir in flour with wooden spoon. Stir in walnuts. Do not overbeat.

• Transfer batter to prepared pan. Bake 30 to 35 minutes or until foggies are just set around edges. They will be moist in centre. Cool 30 minutes in pan on wire rack. Cover pan tightly with aluminium foil. Refrigerate overnight or at least 6 hours.

• Remove foil and run sharp knife around edge of pan. Using two ends of foil as handles, invert foggies onto large plate or cutting board; peel off foil. Invert foggies again onto plate or board. Cut into square or bars.

Makes 2 to 3 dozen.

NANAIMO BARS

Talk about the real McCoy! In the winter of '87, Sun columnist Karen Boulton came back from Vancouver Island with this incredible recipe. Joyce Hardcastle won a bake-off sponsored by local Nanaimo businessmen with these bars. One of Mrs. Hardcastle's tricks is to use good-quality unsalted butter.

FIRST LAYER:

½ cup	unsalted butter	125 mL
¼ cup	granulated sugar	50 mL
5 tbsp	cocoa powder	65 mL
1	egg, beaten	1
1¾ cups	Graham cracker crumbs	425 mL
½ cup	finely chopped almonds	125 mL
1 cup	shredded coconut	250 mL

• Combine butter, sugar and cocoa in top of double boiler. Cook, stirring, over barely simmering water until melted. Add egg. Cook, stirring, until thickened. Remove from heat. Stir in crumbs, almonds and coconut. Press mixture into ungreased 8-inch/2-L square pan. Chill.

SECOND LAYER:

½ cup	unsalted butter (room temperature)	125 mL
3 tbsp	whipping or light cream	45 mL
2 tbsp	vanilla custard powder (e.g. Bird's)	25 mL
2 cups	icing sugar	500 mL

• Cream butter, cream and custard powder together in bowl. Gradually beat in icing sugar until light and fluffy. Spread over chilled first layer. Chill.

THIRD LAYER:

4 oz	semisweet chocolate	125 g
2 tbsp	unsalted butter	25 mL

• Melt chocolate and butter in top of double boiler over barely simmering water. Mix well. Cool to room temperature. Pour evenly over second layer. Smooth top with spatula. Chill. Cut in squares.

Makes 16 to 24.

ROCKY ROAD BARS

The home economists at General Foods came up with this incredible recipe, using every kind of yummy baking ingredient imaginable. The result is a gooey, rich and super-sweet creation that will appeal to the kid in everyone.

½ cup	melted butter	125 mL
1½ cups	Graham cracker crumbs	375 mL
½ cup	smooth or chunky peanut butter	125 mL
3	1-oz/28-g squares semisweet chocolate, melted	3
2 cups	flaked coconut	500 mL
1 cup	chopped unsalted peanuts	250 mL
1½ cups	miniature marshmallows	375 mL
1	300-mL can sweetened condensed milk	1

- Preheat oven to 350°F/180°C.
- Combine butter and crumbs in small bowl until well mixed. Press mixture into 13 × 9-inch/3.5-L baking pan.
- Combine peanut butter and one-third melted chocolate in bowl. Mix well. Mix in coconut. Sprinkle mixture over crumb crust in pan.
- Evenly sprinkle on peanuts, then marshmallows. Drizzle condensed milk evenly on top.
- Bake 25 to 30 minutes or until golden brown. Remove from oven. Drizzle with remaining melted chocolate. Cool before cutting into squares or bars.

Makes 2 to 3 dozen.

OATMEAL TOFFEE SQUARES

These chewy squares are the invention of Kim Quigley, a mother of two who specializes in quick-and-easy baking. Kids will love these. So will adults.

CRUST:

1 cup	all-purpose flour	250 mL
½ cup	butter (room temperature)	125 mL
3 tbsp	granulated sugar	45 mL

- Preheat oven to 350°F/180°C.
- Lightly butter 8-inch/2-L square baking pan.
- Combine crust ingredients in bowl until well mixed. Press into prepared pan. Bake 15 minutes.

TOPPING:

2	eggs, lightly beaten	2
2 tbsp	all-purpose flour	25 mL
1 cup	quick-cooking (not instant) rolled oats	250 mL
1½ cups	brown sugar	375 mL
½ cup	unsweetened coconut	125 mL
½ tsp	vanilla	2 mL

- Combine topping ingredients in bowl. Mix well. Spoon over crust.
- Bake 25 to 30 minutes or until golden brown. Cool. Cut into squares or bars.

Makes 16 to 24.

ANNABEL'S KILLER BROWNIES

Visiting caterer from New Zealand, Annabel Langbein, discovered these at a dinner party in Boston, Massachusetts. The hostess agreed to part with this "killer" recipe, and I'm glad she did. These brownies are everything they're supposed to be, and more! Nut-lovers can add ½ cup/125 mL of their favorite chopped nuts to the batter. For a refreshing mint flavor, add ½ tsp/2 mL peppermint extract along with the vanilla.

1 cup	butter (room temperature)	250 mL
2¼ cups	granulated sugar	550 mL
4	eggs	4
1¼ cups	all-purpose flour	300 mL
5	1-oz/28-g squares unsweetened chocolate, melted and cooled	5
1	175-g package semisweet chocolate chips (1 cup/250 mL)	1
2 tsp	vanilla	10 mL
½ tsp	salt	2 mL

- Preheat oven to 350°F/180°C.
- Lightly butter 13 × 9-inch/3.5-L baking pan.
- Cream butter and sugar until light and fluffy in bowl. Add eggs, one at a time, beating well between each addition. Add flour, melted chocolate, chocolate chips, vanilla and salt. Mix until blended. Pour into prepared pan.
- Bake 40 to 50 minutes or until toothpick inserted comes out clean. Cool in pan. Cut into squares or bars.

Makes 2 to 3 dozen.

No-Bake Brownies

I challenge anyone to guess that these superb brownies are unbaked! Invented by the home economists at Nabisco, they are among the best I've tasted. And making them is so simple, it's child's play.

3 cups	chocolate Graham cracker crumbs	750 mL
1 cup	chopped walnuts	250 mL
½ cup	icing sugar	125 mL
1	350-g package semisweet chocolate chips (2 cups/500 mL)	1
1	160-mL can evaporated milk (2/3 cup/150 mL)	1
1 tsp	vanilla	5 mL
2 tbsp	butter	25 mL

- Line 9-inch/2.5-L square baking pan with aluminium foil. Butter foil.
- Combine crumbs, walnuts and icing sugar in large bowl.
- Melt half of chocolate chips with evaporated milk in saucepan over low heat, stirring constantly, until smooth. Add vanilla. Stir in crumb mixture until well blended. Press firmly into prepared pan.
- Melt remaining chocolate chips with butter in top of double boiler over barely simmering water. Spread evenly over brownie layer. Chill at least 2 hours or overnight. Remove from pan. Peel off foil. Cut into squares or bars.

Makes 16 to 24.

Turtle Squares

Runner-up in Open Kitchen's Squares Bake-Off Contest, these came from Mary Humenik of Toronto. They are chewy, chocolatey, nutty and simply divine!

	CRUST:	
2 cups	all-purpose flour	500 mL
1 cup	firmly packed brown sugar	250 mL
½ cup	butter (room temperature)	125 mL
1 cup	chopped or whole pecans	250 mL

- Preheat oven to 350°F/180°C.
- Combine flour, brown sugar and butter in bowl. Mix with fork or pastry cutter until mixture resembles coarse crumbs. Press into ungreased 13 × 9-inch/3.5-L rectangular baking pan. Sprinkle pecans on top. Press lightly into crust.

TOPPING:

½ cup	butter	125 mL
½ cup	firmly packed brown sugar	125 mL
1	175-g package semisweet chocolate chips (1 cup/250 mL)	1

- Combine butter and brown sugar in heavy saucepan. Cook over medium heat, stirring, until mixture comes to boil. Boil 1 minute. Pour evenly over crust.
- Bake 18 to 20 minutes or until bubbly and golden brown. Remove from oven. Immediately sprinkle with chocolate chips. Let sit 1 to 2 minutes or until chips are melted. Swirl with fork to make zig-zag design. Cool. Cut in squares or bars.

Makes 2 to 3 dozen.

DREAM BARS

Sometimes known as Hello Dollies, these make-in-a-minute bars are a sure hit at any party, pot-luck meal or in junior's lunch bag. As with many sweets, a little goes a long way.

½ cup	melted butter	125 mL
1 cup	Graham cracker crumbs	250 mL
1 cup	flaked or shredded coconut	250 mL
1	175-g package chocolate chips (1 cup/250 mL)	1
1	175-g package butterscotch chips (1 cup/ 250 mL)	1
1¼ cups	chopped walnuts	300 mL
1	300-mL can sweetened condensed milk	1

- Preheat oven to 350°F/180°C.
- Combine butter and crumbs in bowl until mixed. Press mixture into 13 × 9-inch/3.5-L baking pan.
- Combine remaining ingredients in bowl. Spread over crumb crust.
- Bake 30 minutes. Cool. Cut into squares or bars.

Makes 2 to 3 dozen.

PECAN CHOCOLATE CHUNK COOKIES

The winning recipe in Open Kitchen's Chocolate Chip Cookie Contest. It was the brainchild of Esta Wall, who had the idea of breaking a top-quality chocolate bar into chunks.

⅔ cup	coarsely chopped pecans	150 mL
½ cup	butter (room temperature)	125 mL
½ cup	brown sugar	125 mL
¼ cup	granulated sugar	50 mL
1 tsp	vanilla	5 mL
¼ tsp	salt	1 mL
1	egg	1
½ tsp	baking soda	2 mL
1 cup	all-purpose flour	250 mL
12 oz	Lindt or other top-quality bittersweet chocolate, coarsely chopped	375 g

- Preheat oven to 350 °F/180°C.
- Lightly butter cookie sheet.
- Shaking constantly, toast pecans in heavy skillet over low heat until aromatic, about 5 minutes. Cool.
- Combine butter, brown sugar, granulated sugar, vanilla and salt in large bowl. Cream together until light and fluffy. Beat in egg and baking soda. Stir in flour, chocolate and cooled pecans. Shape dough into balls. Place on cookie sheet.
- Bake 10 to 12 minutes. Cool 2 minutes before transferring to wire rack.

Makes about 2 dozen.

BEST BUTTER TARTS

Open Kitchen's contest—Best of the Butter Tarts—got an amazing response. It seems that every family in Ontario has a favorite recipe for this all-Canadian confection. This one from Teresa Almon of Richmond Hill was, after much difficult deliberation, the judges' first choice, Maple syrup and dates are the two "secret" ingredients to this firm butter tart.

PASTRY:

2 cups	all-purpose flour	500 mL
1 tsp	salt	5 mL
1 cup	hard margarine or butter	250 mL
¼ cup	ice-cold water	50 mL

• Sift flour and salt together into bowl. Cut in margarine with two knives or pastry cutter. Add water. Mix with fork until pastry can be gathered into ball. Wrap in plastic wrap. Chill at least 30 minutes.

FILLING:

2	eggs	2
1 cup	brown sugar	250 mL
½ tsp	salt	2 mL
2 tsp	white vinegar	10 mL
½ cup	maple syrup	125 mL
⅓ cup	melted butter	75 mL
⅔ cup	chopped walnuts	150 mL
½ cup	currants	125 mL
½ cup	chopped dates	125 mL

• Preheat oven to 350°F/180°C.

• Beat eggs in bowl. Gradually add sugar. Beat until light and fluffy. Add salt, vinegar, maple syrup and melted butter. Mix just until combined. Stir in walnuts, currants and dates.

• Roll out dough. Line tart tins with dough. Fill two-thirds full with filling. Bake 25 to 30 minutes or until firm.

Makes 2 to 2½ dozen.

CHOCOLATE TRUFFLES

Use good-quality imported chocolate (such as Lindt's bittersweet) for these melt-in-the-mouth lovelies. Perfect anytime you want to celebrate or give a gift to someone special. These appeared in "Feeding Bawdy and Soul" in February, 1987—an article in which I offered recipes for amorous enticement at Valentine's.

12 oz	semisweet chocolate, chopped	375 g
½ cup	whipping cream	125 mL
3 tbsp	brandy	45 mL
½ cup	cocoa powder	125 mL

• Combine chocolate, cream and brandy in top of double boiler. Melt over barely simmering water, stirring occasionally, until well blended. Transfer to bowl. Chill until firm.

• Scoop up chocolate mixture with melon baller. Shape into bite-sized balls. Roll in cocoa.

Makes about 40.

PECAN LACE COOKIES

Rose Murray, cookbook author, food consultant, food writer and cook par excellence, contributed these fabulous cookies to the Sun food section in the fall of '85. I frequently make these in cup shapes for dinner parties and fill them with mousse or ice cream topped with fruit sauce. They are also superb made into flat cookies as a sidekick for fruit salad, sherbet or ice cream.

½ cup	unsalted butter	125 mL
½ cup	firmly packed brown sugar	125 mL
½ cup	corn syrup	125 mL
1 cup	all-purpose flour	250 mL
½ tsp	vanilla	2 mL
¾ cup	finely chopped pecans	175 mL

- Preheat oven to 325°F/160°C.
- Generously butter two cookie sheets.
- Combine butter, brown sugar and corn syrup in heavy saucepan. Stir until mixed. Place over medium heat; bring to boil, stirring. Cook just until sugar is dissolved. Remove from heat. Stir in flour, vanilla and pecans. Blend well.
- Drop by scant teaspoonfuls 4 inches/10 cm apart on prepared cookie sheet. Cookies will spread during baking.
- Bake 8 to 10 minutes or until golden brown. Remove from oven. Cool on pans 2 minutes. Transfer cookies to wire rack. Cookies must cool perfectly flat. Store in airtight containers with wax paper between layers.

Makes 4 to 5 dozen.

NOTE: To make cookie cups, follow above recipe but instead of dropping batter by teaspoonfuls, use 2 tbsp/25 mL batter for each cookie. Bake only three at a time, cool a few seconds and then, working quickly, drape each cookie over ½ cup/125 mL custard cup or place in large muffin tin to make into cup shapes.

MARY MACLEOD'S SHORTBREAD

There are many Torontonians for whom Christmas would be incomplete without a batch of Mary MacLeod's famous shortbread. MacLeod worked for years on a family recipe from her native Scotland until she perfected it. This is one version made with brown sugar. Easy to make, it gets my vote for the quintessential shortbread.

2½ cups	cake and pastry flour	625 mL
⅔ cup	firmly packed dark brown sugar	150 mL
1 cup	salted butter (room temperature)	250 mL

- Preheat oven to 300°F/150°C.
- Sift flour and sugar together in food processor or large bowl. Add butter. Process in food processor or rub butter into flour mixture with hands until mixture resembles coarse crumbs. Gather mixture into ball. Place on counter or wooden board. Gently knead dough with heel of hand 5 minutes. Dough should not be too sticky. Add a little more flour if necessary.
- Divide dough in half. Shape each half into flat disc ½ inch/1 cm thick. Prick all over with fork. Bake 1 hour or until barely colored around edges.

Makes two rounds about 7 inches/17 cm in diameter.

RICE FLOUR SHORTBREAD

In the winter of 1985, Open Kitchen's Surefire Shortbread Contest drew a huge response. This recipe from Lori Dunne of North York, a runner-up, uses rice flour, which produces a very delicate shortbread.

2 cups	butter (room temperature)	500 mL
½ cup	brown sugar	125 mL
1 cup	rice flour	250 mL
3 cups	sifted all-purpose flour	750 mL
	Granulated or fruit sugar for sprinkling	

- Preheat oven to 275°F/140°C.
- Cream butter and sugar together until light and fluffy. Add flours. Blend first with wooden spoon and then with hands until dough is smooth. Turn onto floured surface. Knead 1 minute. Pat and roll with rolling pin until ½ inch/1 cm thick. Cut into squares or desired shape. Sprinkle with sugar.
- Place on ungreased cookie sheet. Bake 25 to 30 minutes or until barely browned around edges.

Makes about 4 dozen.

SHORTBREAD SNOWMEN

Jan Poon, food stylist, artist, cookbook author and all-round "Renaissance woman," is one of the most creative cooks I know. These snowmen are fiddly to make, but taste and look so magnificent that I recommend you gather up some kids for an afternoon and give this fabulous recipe a try.

SHORTBREAD:

1 cup	butter (room temperature)	250 mL
½ cup	icing sugar	125 mL
1 tsp	vanilla	5 mL
1 cup	ground almonds	250 mL
2 cups	all-purpose flour	500 mL
27	maraschino cherries	27

• Preheat oven to 325°F/160°C.

• Lightly butter two cookie sheets. Dust with flour.

• Cream butter until fluffy. Beat in sugar and vanilla. Mix in almonds and flour, stirring only enough to blend ingredients completely. Gather dough into ball.

• Divide dough into two equal halves on floured surface. Form each into a long cylinder about 15 inches/38 cm long. Cut one cylinder into 18 equal segments. Form each segment into a ball encasing a single maraschino cherry. Place balls 1 inch/2 cm apart on prepared cookie sheets.

• Cut remaining cylinder into 36 segments. Cut remaining cherries in half. Form 18 segments into balls, each encasing a halved cherry. Place on prepared cookie sheet.

• Form small balls with remaining segments of dough. Squeeze sides of each ball together slightly. (These will be the snowmen's top hats.)

• Bake cookies 25 to 30 minutes or until bottoms are lightly browned. (Smaller cookies will be ready before larger ones.) Cool on wire racks.

ICING:

½ cup	butter (room temperature)	125 mL
1 cup	icing sugar	250 mL
¼ tsp	vanilla	1 mL
	Food coloring of choice	
2	40-g chocolate bars or equivalent chocolate chips	2

• Cream butter until fluffy. Beat in icing sugar and vanilla. Add a few drops of food coloring; beat until blended.

• Melt chocolate bars in top of double boiler over barely simmering water. Dip unfilled cookie segments in melted chocolate, one at a time, to coat. Place on greased cookie sheet. Let harden in fridge at least 15 minutes. These will be snowmen's hats. Reserve remaining melted chocolate for eyes and buttons.

• To ice cookies, fill piping bag fitted with small round tip with icing. Squeeze about ¼ tsp/1 mL icing on top of each of large cookies. Place smaller cookie on top. Place another drop of icing on top of smaller cookie and attach chocolate-covered hat (see diagram).

• Draw scarf with icing. Using a toothpick, draw eyes, nose and buttons with reserved melted chocolate.

Makes 18 snowmen.

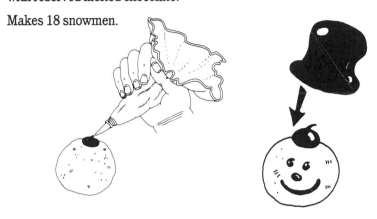

ALMOND TOFFEE BARS

It's almost impossible to stop eating these crunchy cookies! Sometimes called Fat Alberts, these bars are made with Graham crackers coated in toffee and nuts. Barbara Anderson contributed this recipe to Open Kitchen, and I don't know whether to thank or curse her, for introducing me to these addictive confections!

30	Graham crackers, approx.	30
1½ cups	sliced almonds	375 mL
1 cup	butter	250 mL
1 cup	brown sugar	250 mL

• Preheat oven to 400°F/200°C.

• Line cookie sheet with Graham crackers, cutting and fitting crackers so that they completely cover cookie sheet with no gaps in between. Sprinkle 1 cup/250 mL almonds over crackers.

• Melt butter in saucepan. Stir in brown sugar; bring to boil. Cook over medium-low heat 2 to 3 minutes, stirring constantly. Pour evenly over crackers. Sprinkle remaining almonds on top.

• Bake 7 to 8 minutes or until bubbling all over. Cool a few minutes. Cut into bars along edges of crackers. Remove from pan immediately.

Makes about 2 to 3 dozen.

PEANUTTY CHOCOLATE CHUNK COOKIES

A crunchy, melt-in-the-mouth cookie with the double whammy of peanuts and peanut butter from pastry chef Andrew Malcolmson. For a shortcut, you could use chocolate chips instead of breaking a bar into chunks.

1 cup	butter (room temperature)	250 mL
1½ cups	brown sugar	375 mL
¾ cup	crunchy peanut butter	175 mL
2	eggs	2
1 tsp	vanilla	5 mL
2½ cups	all-purpose flour	625 mL
1 tsp	baking soda	5 mL
6 oz	top-quality semisweet chocolate, chopped into chunks (about 1 cup/250 mL)	175 g
1 cup	unsalted peanuts	250 mL

- Preheat oven to 350°F/180°C.
- Lightly butter cookie sheet.
- Cream butter and sugar in bowl until fluffy. Add peanut butter. Beat until well blended. Add eggs and vanilla. Beat until light and fluffy.
- Sift flour and baking soda into separate bowl. Add to butter mixture. Mix well. Stir in chocolate chunks. Place mixture by spoonfuls on prepared cookie sheet. Sprinkle a few peanuts on each cookie. Press lightly with fork or fingers to flatten slightly.
- Bake 10 to 12 minutes or until golden brown.

Makes about 4 dozen.

OATMEAL CHOCOLATE CHIPPERS

These great-tasting high-fibre cookies are made with oatmeal, wholewheat flour and nuts. The recipe comes from Carol White, food writer, cookbook editor and product developer for food companies. Perfect for brown-bagging it at school, the office or anywhere that snacking is in order.

1 cup	butter (room temperature)	250 mL
¾ cup	brown sugar	175 mL
¾ cup	granulated sugar	175 mL
2	eggs	2
1½ cups	wholewheat flour	375 mL

1 tsp	baking soda	5 mL
1 tsp	salt	5 mL
1	350-g package semisweet chocolate chips (2 cups/500 mL)	1
2 cups	quick-cooking (not instant) rolled oats	500 mL
1 tsp	vanilla	5 mL
1 cup	chopped walnuts or pecans	250 mL

- Preheat oven to 375°F/190°C. Lightly butter cookie sheet.
- Cream butter and sugars in large bowl or in food processor until light and fluffy. Beat in eggs.
- Sift flour, baking soda and salt together into separate bowl.
- Beat dry ingredients into creamed mixture. Stir in chocolate chips, oats, vanilla and nuts. Mix well. Drop by spoonfuls onto prepared cookie sheet.
- Bake 8 to 10 minutes or until golden brown. Cool on wire rack.

Makes 3 dozen.

ALMOND TUILES

Another super recipe from Sun *recipe tester, Janet Cornish. These beautifully plain, nutty cookies get their name from those curved tiled rooftops common in the south of France. Ideal with ice cream or fruit salad.*

½ cup	granulated sugar	125 mL
⅓ cup	egg whites (about 3)	75 mL
½ tsp	lemon juice	2 mL
⅓ cup	all-purpose flour	75 mL
¼ cup	melted butter	50 mL
½ cup	ground almonds	125 mL
1 tbsp	grated lemon rind	15 mL
¾ cup	sliced almonds	175 mL

- Preheat oven to 325°F/160°C.
- Lightly butter two cookie sheets.
- Beat sugar, egg whites and lemon juice in bowl until foamy. Add flour, melted butter, ground almonds and lemon rind, mixing thoroughly.
- Drop batter by teaspoonfuls onto prepared cookie sheet, allowing no more than 8 cookies per sheet. Sprinkle with sliced almonds.
- Bake 8 to 10 minutes or until edges are golden brown. Remove one at a time. Drape over rolling pin or bottle. Cool completely on rolling pin to form concave cookies.

Makes about 20.

FRUITY CRESCENT COOKIES

Cookbook author and cooking teacher Sandra Temes contributed this recipe as a Hannukah dessert idea when she was Cook of the Week in December, 1985. I became an instant convert when I tasted the freshly baked samples of these buttery, fruity crescents. Take your time and follow the diagram when shaping the dough into crescents; you'll find they're actually quite simple to make.

CRESCENTS:

⅔ cup	sour cream	150 mL
1	egg yolk	1
2 cups	all-purpose flour	500 mL
3 tbsp	granulated sugar	45 mL
1 cup	unsalted butter, cold	250 mL

• Lightly beat sour cream and egg yolk in small bowl. Set aside for 15 minutes.

• Combine flour and sugar in large bowl. Cut in butter with two knives or pastry cutter until mixture resembles coarse crumbs. Add sour cream mixture. Stir with fork until dough sticks together. Transfer dough with floured hands to plastic wrap. Shape into ball. Refrigerate at least 8 hours but not more than 2 days.

FILLING:

½ cup	chopped pecans, walnuts or hazelnuts	125 mL
½ cup	shredded coconut	125 mL
¼ cup	raisins	50 mL
	Granulated sugar for dusting	
¼ to ½ cup	apricot, raspberry or favorite jam	50 to 125 mL
1	egg white, beaten	1

• Remove dough from fridge 45 minutes before assembling cookies.

• Combine pecans, coconut and raisins in small bowl. Mix well.

• When dough is pliable, divide into four equal parts. Roll each piece into a circle about 1/8 inch/3 mm thick on floured and sugared surface. Dust with sugar. Cut into 12 pie-shaped wedges (see diagram). Place ¼ tsp/1 mL jam at widest edge of each wedge. Add a little filling. Roll from widest edge to point. Bend ends forward to form crescent. Transfer to two ungreased cookie sheets. Place seam underneath to prevent unwinding during baking. Chill at least 30 minutes.

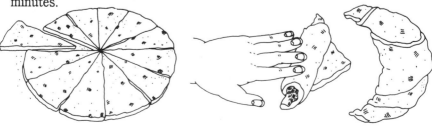

- Preheat oven to 375°F/190°C.
- Brush crescents with beaten egg white. Bake 20 to 25 minutes or until golden brown.

Makes 4 dozen.

NOTE: These can be frozen on cookie sheets before baking. When solid, transfer to plastic bag and re-freeze. Thaw in fridge and brush with beaten egg white just before baking.

JANET'S FAMOUS FLORENTINES

This recipe for one of my favorite cookies is the invention of Sun recipe tester, Janet Cornish. Her version of this lacy, chocolate-coated munchie laden with fruit and nuts even has my mother's beat! Perfect with tea or as an accompaniment to fruit salad as a dinner finale.

3 cups	sliced almonds	750 mL
½ cup	chopped candied citrus peel	125 mL
½ cup	chopped candied cherries	125 mL
½ cup	unsalted butter	125 mL
1⅓ cups	granulated sugar	325 mL
¼ cup	honey	50 mL
8 oz	good-quality semisweet or bittersweet chocolate, melted	250 g

- Preheat oven to 350°F/180°C.
- Line cookie sheet with parchment or wax paper.
- Combine almonds, peel and cherries in bowl.
- Combine butter, sugar and honey in heavy saucepan. Bring to boil, stirring constantly. Cook until mixture reaches about 234°F/112°C or soft ball stage (when dropped into very cold water, syrup forms a soft ball which flattens on removal from water). Remove from heat; stir in almond mixture.
- Drop by spoonfuls onto prepared cookie sheet, about 3 inches/7 cm apart. Bake 5 to 6 minutes or until cookies start to spread. Remove from oven. Shape cookies into rounds with cookie cutter or drinking glass. Return to oven. Bake just until cookies start to spread and are caramel-colored, about 5 minutes. Remove from oven. Re-shape again with cookie cutter or drinking glass. Cool. Brush one side of each cookie with melted chocolate. Cool completely.

Makes 2 dozen.

HAZELNUT CRESCENTS

My mother, who grew up in Eastern Europe where these cookies are a festive tradition, has been making them every Christmas as long as I can remember. They are truly delicious and a cinch to make. You can make them well ahead of the frantic holiday rush and freeze or store them (without the icing sugar dusting) in an airtight container.

1 cup	butter (room temperature)	250 mL
½ cup	icing sugar	125 mL
1 tsp	vanilla	5 mL
1 tsp	cold water	5 mL
1 cup	hazelnuts (filberts), finely ground	250 mL
2 cups	all-purpose flour	500 mL
½ to 1 cup	icing sugar for dusting	125 to 250 mL

- Preheat oven to 350°F/180°C.
- Cream butter and icing sugar together in bowl until light and fluffy. Stir in vanilla and water until blended. Stir in hazelnuts. Gradually stir in flour. Mix well.
- Shape teaspoonfuls of dough into crescents with hands. Place on ungreased cookie sheets. Bake 10 to 12 minutes or until lightly browned on bottom. Cool slightly. Roll in icing sugar.

Makes about 4 dozen.

NOTE: If serving same day, roll in icing sugar while still warm. If baking ahead, store in airtight container and roll in sifted icing sugar just before serving.

PECAN PUFFS

Food writer Jane Rodmell put her talents to excellent use when she and her partners opened that wonderful Toronto bakery, All the Best Breads. This melt-in-the-mouth shortbread-like cookie with the crunch of pecans is particularly popular there at Christmas, but a big seller year round.

1 cup	pecans	250 mL
1 cup	unsalted butter (room temperature)	250 mL
¼ cup	granulated sugar	50 mL
2 cups	all-purpose flour	500 mL
¼ tsp	salt	1 mL
2 tsp	vanilla	10 mL
¾ cup	icing sugar for dusting	175 mL

- Preheat oven to 350°F/180°C.
- Spread pecans on cookie sheet. Toast in oven 7 minutes. Cool. Chop in food processor to form rough crumbs.
- Cream butter and sugar in bowl until light and fluffy.
- Toss flour with salt in separate bowl. Add to creamed mixture. Stir in vanilla and toasted nuts. Mix well.
- Form dough into small balls the size of a teaspoon. Place on ungreased cookie sheet. Bake 20 to 25 minutes until cookies are golden brown on bottom.

Makes about 3 ½ dozen.

NOTE: If serving cookies the same day, dust with icing sugar while still warm. If making ahead, store in airtight container and dust with sifted icing sugar just before serving.

WELSH CAKES

Vera Jones donated this excellent recipe to Open Kitchen in March, 1986. These buttery, scone-like griddle cakes are a tradition in her native Wales and could easily become a favorite tea-time pastry in your house. Serve with homemade jam, or fruit preserves and cream if your waistline can take it!

3¾ cups	cake and pastry flour	925 mL
¾ cup	granulated sugar	175 mL
1 tsp	baking powder	5 mL
1 tsp	ground nutmeg	5 mL
pinch	salt	pinch
¼ cup	cold butter, cut in chunks	50 mL
1 cup	hard margarine, cut in chunks	250 mL
1 cup	currants	250 mL
3	eggs, lightly beaten	3

- Combine dry ingredients in food processor. Add butter and margarine. Process until mixture resembles coarse crumbs. (You could also do this by cutting butter and margarine into flour mixture with two knives or pastry cutter.) Transfer to bowl. Mix in currants and eggs, stirring until mixture forms soft dough.
- Roll out on floured surface until ¼ inch/5 mm thick. Cut into rounds with 2-inch/5-cm cutter.
- Heat ungreased heavy skillet or griddle over medium-high heat. Add cakes; cook until golden brown on each side, about 1 minute per side.

Makes about 4 dozen. Store in airtight container in fridge.

RAISIN SCONES

This recipe appeared in an article called "Romancing the Scone" in the summer of '86. One of the best culinary ideas to come out of the British penchant for afternoon tea, this is a top-notch version from the editor of Woman's Day magazine, Elizabeth Alston. Serve with good homemade jam or preserves and clotted (Devon) cream.

2 cups	all-purpose flour	500 mL
2 tsp	baking powder	10 mL
½ tsp	baking soda	2 mL
½ tsp	ground nutmeg	2 mL
½ tsp	salt	2 mL
½ cup	cold unsalted butter, cut in pieces	125 mL
1 cup	raisins	250 mL
2 tbsp	granulated sugar	25 mL
1	egg, separated	1
¾ cup	buttermilk or unflavored yogurt	175 mL
	Granulated sugar for dusting	

- Preheat oven to 375°F/190°C.
- Combine flour, baking powder, baking soda, nutmeg and salt in large bowl. Cut in butter with two knives or pastry cutter until mixture resembles coarse crumbs. Add raisins and sugar. Mix well.
- Whisk egg yolk and buttermilk with fork or whisk in small bowl until blended. Pour into flour mixture. Stir with fork until soft dough forms. Turn onto floured surface. Knead 10 to 12 times. Cut in half. Shape each half into ball. Pat each ball into a circle 6 inches/15 cm in diameter. Score top with knife to form six wedges. Brush with egg white; dust with sugar.
- Bake rounds on cookie sheet 20 minutes or until golden brown.

Makes 12 wedge-shaped scones.

NOTE: If desired, cut dough into cookie-sized rounds 1 inch/2 cm thick instead of making large rounds.

CAKES

INCREDIBLE CARROT CAKE

Sun columnist Karen Boulton came up with this ultimate version of an all-time favorite for a 1986 Valentine's story called "Sweet Memories." It's no wonder that this moist dessert, which combines the nutrition of carrots with that "spoonful of sugar," has not gone out of fashion since the 1970s, when carrot cake was all the culinary rage. This makes a big cake—perfect for birthdays, parties or, of course, Valentine's!

CAKE:

1 cup	chopped walnuts or hazelnuts	250 mL
4	eggs	4
1 cup	granulated sugar	250 mL
1 cup	dark brown sugar	250 mL
1½ cups	vegetable oil	375 mL
2 cups	all-purpose flour	500 mL
2 tsp	baking powder	10 mL
1½ tsp	baking soda	7 mL
2 tbsp	ground cinnamon	25 mL
1 tsp	salt	5 mL
2½ cups	grated carrots	625 mL
1 cup	unsweetened crushed pineapple, undrained	250 mL
1 tsp	vanilla	5 mL
1 cup	raisins (optional)	250 mL

- Preheat oven to 350°F/180°C.
- Lightly butter and flour three 9-inch/1.5-L round cake pans.
- Shaking constantly, toast nuts in heavy skillet over low heat until aromatic, about 5 minutes. Remove from heat.
- Beat eggs in large bowl. Add sugars and oil. Beat until light and creamy.
- Sift flour, baking powder, baking soda, cinnamon and salt into separate bowl.
- Add dry ingredients to egg mixture. Beat until blended. Do not overmix. Stir in carrots, pineapple, toasted nuts, vanilla and raisins. Divide batter evenly among prepared pans.
- Bake 30 to 40 minutes or until toothpick inserted comes out clean. Cool 5 minutes in pan. Invert onto wire racks. Cool completely.

CREAM CHEESE ICING:

1 lb	cream cheese (room temperature)	500 g
½ cup	unsalted butter (room temperature)	125 mL
	Rind of 1 lemon	
2 tbsp	lemon juice	25 mL
2 cups	icing sugar, sifted	500 mL

- Beat cream cheese until soft and fluffy with electric mixer. Add butter, rind and juice. Beat until blended. Add icing sugar. Beat on low speed until incorporated. Beat on high speed until smooth. Spread over cooled cake.

SOUR CREAM COFFEE CAKE

This recipe, from Sue Devor of Sweet Sue Pastries in Toronto, can be whipped up in no time for tea-time guests who drop by on a weekend afternoon. It's also great on a dessert table at parties. Substitute unflavored yogurt—the low-fat kind if desired—for a healthier, tasty rendition of one of my favorite confections.

TOPPING:

½ cup	dark brown sugar	125 mL
2 tsp	ground cinnamon	10 mL
1 tbsp	cocoa powder	15 mL
3 tbsp	vegetable oil	45 mL
1 tbsp	chopped nuts (optional)	15 mL

- Preheat oven to 350°F/180°C.
- Lightly butter and flour 9-inch/3-L springform tube or Bundt pan.
- Combine topping ingredients in bowl. Set aside.

CAKE:

2	eggs	2
1 cup	granulated sugar	250 mL
½ cup	vegetable oil	125 mL
1½ cups	all-purpose flour	375 mL
1 tbsp	baking powder	15 mL
⅓ cup	unsweetened orange juice	75 mL
¼ cup	sour cream or unflavored yogurt	50 mL
½ tsp	vanilla	2 mL

- Beat eggs, sugar and oil in large bowl until light and creamy.
- Sift flour and baking powder into separate bowl.
- Add flour mixture, orange juice, sour cream and vanilla to egg mixture. Mix until blended. Do not overmix. Pour half of batter into prepared pan. Sprinkle with half of topping mixture. Pour on remaining batter. Sprinkle on remaining topping.
- Bake 35 to 40 minutes or until toothpick inserted comes out clean.

YOUR BASIC CHEESECAKE

This recipe has a special place in my heart, since it was part of the very first article I wrote when I joined the Sun *as food editor in October, 1983. It is also one of the best cheesecakes I have tasted. Easy to make, the sour cream topping gives a pretty, smooth glaze that you can crown with whatever fresh berries are in season. I also offer a recipe for raspberry topping, although I prefer this cake just topped with fresh berries. It is well worth splurging on top-quality cream cheese for this cake. I recommend Mandel's for anyone living in Toronto.*

CRUST:

3 tbsp	melted butter	45 mL
¾ cup	Graham cracker crumbs	175 mL
1 tbsp	granulated sugar	15 mL

• Combine crust ingredients in bowl. Press into 9-inch/2.5-L springform pan. Chill.

FILLING:

1 lb	cream cheese (room temperature)	500 g
3	eggs	3
⅔ cup	granulated sugar	150 mL
	Grated rind of 1 lemon	
2 tbsp	lemon juice	25 mL
½ cup	sour cream	125 mL

• Preheat oven to 350°F/180°C.
• Beat cheese in bowl until fluffy. Add eggs, sugar, lemon rind and juice. Beat until smooth. Stir in sour cream. Beat until blended. Pour batter onto chilled crust.
• Bake 30 to 35 minutes or until cake is puffed and trembles just slightly when shaken.

TOPPING:

1 cup	sour cream	250 mL
3 tbsp	granulated sugar	45 mL
2 tbsp	lemon juice	25 mL

• Combine topping ingredients in bowl. Spread evenly over cake. Return to oven 5 minutes. Cool to room temperature. Refrigerate overnight. top with fresh berries, fine shreds of lemon rind or raspberry glaze.

RASPBERRY GLAZE:

1	300-g package frozen unsweetened raspberries	1
3 tbsp	granulated sugar	45 mL
2 tbsp	cornstarch	25 mL

- Place raspberries in strainer over bowl; thaw. Drain well, reserving liquid. Measure drained liquid; add enough cold water to make 1 cup.
- Combine sugar and cornstarch in separate bowl. Add 2 tbsp/25 mL raspberry juice. Stir to make smooth paste. Set aside.
- Bring remaining raspberry juice to boil in small saucepan. Whisk in cornstarch mixture; return to boil. Whisk until thickened. Cool. Stir in raspberries. Spoon over cheesecake.

NOTE: The raspberry glaze, which should be made in advance so it has time to cool, can be served on top of the whole cake or in a separate dish on side, to be poured on as desired.

RUM CAKE

My psychologist friend Sandy Wiseman contributed this fantastic recipe to a Hallowe'en article called "Food with Spirit." The secret to this quick and easy cake really is "in the pudding." It's ideal for party buffets.

1	520-g package golden cake mix	1
1	92-g package instant vanilla pudding	1
4	eggs	4
½ cup	vegetable oil	125 mL
½ cup	amber rum	125 mL
½ cup	water	125 mL

- Preheat oven to 350°F/180°C.
- Lightly butter and flour 10-inch/3-L tube or Bundt springform pan.
- Combine all ingredients in large bowl. Beat with wooden spoon 2 minutes. Pour into prepared pan.
- Bake 45 to 55 minutes or until toothpick inserted comes out clean. Ten minutes before cake is ready, prepare glaze.

	GLAZE:	
¼ cup	amber rum	50 mL
¼ cup	water	50 mL
1 cup	brown sugar	250 mL
¼ cup	butter	50 mL
	Icing sugar for dusting	

- Combine rum, water, brown sugar and butter in small saucepan. Bring to boil. Boil 3 minutes. Spoon very slowly over hot cake, pulling cake gently away from sides of pan to let glaze drizzle down sides. Cool. Remove cake from pan. Dust with sifted icing sugar just before serving.

CHOCOLATE ESPRESSO CHEESECAKE

As rich as they come, this dessert takes the cake for smoothness and superb flavor. This recipe, from the now-defunct Basie's restaurant in Toronto, was the creation of owner Jim Poulos and his wife, Athena. It's so good, you'll only need a sliver! If you cannot find chocolate Graham cracker crumbs, grind chocolate wafers in the food processor until crumb-like.

CRUST:

1¼ cups	chocolate Graham cracker crumbs	300 mL
¼ cup	granulated sugar	50 mL
¼ tsp	ground cinnamon	1 mL
⅓ cup	melted butter	75 mL

• Combine crust ingredients in small bowl. Press into bottom and slightly up sides of 9-inch/2.5-L springform pan. Chill.

FILLING:

8 oz	semisweet chocolate	250 g
1½ lb	cream cheese (room temperature)	750 g
1 cup	granulated sugar	250 mL
3	eggs	3
1 cup	sour cream	250 mL
1 tsp	vanilla	5 mL
½ cup	espresso or very strong coffee, cooled	125 mL
	Semisweet chocolate shavings for garnish	

• Preheat oven to 350°F/180°C.

• Melt chocolate in top of double boiler over barely simmering water. Cool to lukewarm.

• Beat cream cheese, sugar and eggs in large bowl until smooth. Add melted chocolate, sour cream, vanilla and coffee. Stir until blended. Pour into prepared crust.

• Bake 1 hour or until cake is puffed and trembles just slightly when shaken. Cool to room temperature. Refrigerate overnight. Garnish with chocolate shavings.

CHOCOLATE WHISKY CAKE

Sue Devor of Sweet Sue Pastries has been putting together some of Toronto's top confections for many years. This dark, rich cake laced with whisky is a chocoholic's dream. A dense rather than airy cake, it will be fairly shallow when baked.

CAKE:

7 oz	semisweet chocolate	200 g
3 tbsp	water	45 mL
½ cup	butter	125 mL
3	eggs, separated	3
⅔ cup	granulated sugar	150 mL
¼ cup	all-purpose flour	50 mL
⅔ cup	ground almonds	150 mL
¼ cup	whisky or rum	50 mL
	Semisweet chocolate curls or shavings for garnish	

- Preheat oven to 375°F/190°C.
- Lightly grease 9-inch/1.5-L round cake pan. Line bottom with wax paper. Lightly grease and flour paper-lined bottom and sides of pan.
- Melt chocolate with water in top of double boiler over barely simmering water. Remove from heat. Stir in butter.
- Beat egg yolks with sugar in bowl until light and fluffy. Stir in chocolate mixture.
- Combine flour and ground almonds in separate bowl. Stir into chocolate/egg mixture. Stir in whisky.
- Beat egg whites in separate bowl until stiff peaks form. Fold gently into chocolate batter. Pour into prepared pan.
- Bake 40 minutes or until toothpick inserted comes out clean. Cool 10 minutes. Turn onto serving platter. When cool, pour on glaze.

CHOCOLATE GLAZE:

4 oz	semisweet chocolate	125 g
2 tbsp	whipping cream	25 mL

- Melt chocolate in top of double boiler over barely simmering water. Remove from heat. Stir in cream. Spread evenly over cooled cake. Garnish with chocolate shavings.

TRIPLE CHOCOLATE CAKE

My excuse for using this terrific recipe was an article I wrote in July of '86 called "Crazy Mixed-up Food." The photo that accompanied the recipes (all based on packaged foods) was of that "wild and crazy" comedy duo from Australia—Los Trios Ringbarkus. Their act might have been crazy, but using mixes to come up with this incredible cake makes darned good sense! From the people at Duncan Hines.

CAKE:

⅔ cup	slivered almonds	150 mL
1	520-g package devil's food chocolate cake mix	1
1	113-g package instant chocolate pudding mix	1
1 cup	sour cream or unflavored yogurt	250 mL
½ cup	vegetable oil	125 mL
4	eggs	4
2 tbsp	almond or other nut liqueur	25 mL
½ tsp	almond extract	2 mL
2 cups	semisweet chocolate chips	500 mL

- Preheat oven to 350°F/180°C.
- Lightly grease and flour 10-inch/3-L springform tube or Bundt pan.
- Shaking constantly, toast almonds in heavy skillet over low heat until golden brown, about 5 minutes. Remove from heat.
- Combine cake mix, pudding mix, sour cream, oil, eggs, liqueur and extract in large bowl. Beat with electric mixer at medium speed 2 minutes. Stir in ½ cup/125 mL toasted almonds and the chocolate chips. Pour into prepared pan.
- Bake 55 to 60 minutes or until toothpick inserted comes out clean. Cool in pan 10 minutes. Remove from pan. Invert onto wire rack. Cool. Top with glaze.

GLAZE:

4 oz	semisweet chocolate	125 g
3 tbsp	butter	45 mL
2 tbsp	almond liqueur	25 mL
1 tsp	vegetable oil	5 mL

- Melt chocolate and butter in top of double boiler over barely simmering water. Stir in liqueur and oil. Spoon glaze over cooled cake. Garnish with remaining toasted almonds.

CHOCOLATE MOUSSE CAKE

Another superb cake recipe from the Valentine's story of '86—"Sweet Memories." To me, chocolate mousse cake symbolizes the taste in sweets for this decade. More time-consuming to make than most, this cake is definitely worth the effort. The perfect companion to coffee and liqueur, it is chocolate heaven, from its light-as-air top to crispy bottom. If chocolate Graham cracker crumbs are unavailable, grind chocolate wafers in the food processor until crumb-like.

CRUST:

3 cups	chocolate Graham cracker crumbs	750 mL
½ cup	melted butter	125 mL
1¼ tsp	instant coffee powder	7 mL

• Combine crust ingredients in bowl. Press into bottom and three-quarters way up sides of 10-inch/3-L springform pan. Chill.

FILLING:

1 lb	semisweet chocolate	500 g
2	whole eggs	2
4	eggs, separated	4
3 tbsp	dark rum or brandy (optional)	45 mL
2 cups	whipping cream	500 mL
⅓ cup	icing sugar	75 mL

• Melt chocolate in top of double boiler over barely simmering water. Cool to lukewarm. Transfer to large bowl. Add whole eggs, yolks and rum; beat until smooth.
• Whip cream with icing sugar in separate bowl until soft peaks form.
• Beat egg whites in another bowl until stiff but not dry.
• Stir a little whipped cream and beaten egg white into chocolate mixture. Fold in remaining cream and egg whites. Turn into prepared pan. Chill at least 6 hours.

TOPPING:

1 cup	whipping cream	250 mL
1 tbsp	granulated sugar	15 mL
	Semisweet chocolate curls or shavings for garnish	

• Whip cream and sugar in small bowl until soft peaks form.
• Remove sides of pan containing mousse. Spread half of whipped cream topping over mousse. Pipe rosettes decoratively on top of cake with remaining whipped cream. Garnish with chocolate curls or shavings.

CRUNCHY-TOPPED PARADISE CAKE

Food aficionado/caterer Jackie McCarten contributed this recipe to the Sun food section as a super item to take to the cottage. Easy to transport in its baking pan, this is a truly upscale snacking cake. Lie in the sun and nibble on this—and you'll know what paradise is!

2½ cups	all-purpose flour	625 mL
2 cups	granulated sugar	500 mL
1½ tsp	baking powder	7 mL
2 tsp	baking soda	10 mL
1 tsp	salt	5 mL
2 tsp	ground cinnamon	10 mL
1 cup	vegetable oil	250 mL
4	eggs	4
3	ripe bananas, mashed	3
1	14-oz/398-mL can unsweetened crushed pineapple, undrained	1
1½ tsp	vanilla	7 mL

- Preheat oven to 350°F/180°C.
- Lightly butter 13 × 9-inch/3.5-L rectangular baking pan.
- Combine flour, sugar, baking powder, baking soda, salt and cinnamon in large bowl. Add remaining ingredients. Beat with electric mixer on medium speed 1 minute. Pour batter into prepared pan. Bake 1 hour or until toothpick comes out clean. Cool in pan on wire rack 5 minutes.
- Preheat broiler.

CRUNCHY TOPPING:

⅓ cup	butter (room temperature)	75 mL
1 cup	brown sugar	250 mL
¾ cup	shredded coconut	175 mL
½ cup	chopped nuts (walnuts, almonds, etc.)	125 mL

- Cream butter and sugar together in bowl until fluffy. Add coconut and nuts. Mix well. Spread over hot cake. Place 6 inches/15 cm below broiler. Broil until bubbly and brown, about 3 minutes. Let cake cool in pan. To serve, cut in squares.

APPLE BRETON

This wonderful cake is actually a rich, soft-pastried pie. The tartness of the apple offsets the sweet, buttery crust magnificently. This version of a French classic came from Annabel Langbein, a caterer and food columnist from New Zealand, who stopped by Toronto in 1985 long enough for the Sun *food section to snaffle this top-notch recipe!*

CRUST:

1 cup	butter (room temperature)	250 mL
1 cup	granulated sugar	250 mL
1 tsp	vanilla	5 mL
1 tbsp	lemon juice	15 mL
4	egg yolks	4
2¾ cups	all-purpose flour	675 mL
1	egg yolk, lightly beaten, for brushing pastry	1

• Cream butter and sugar in bowl until light and fluffy. Beat in vanilla and lemon juice. Beat in egg yolks, one at a time, until smooth. Mix in flour. Don't overmix. Gather dough into ball. Wrap in plastic wrap. Chill while making filling.

FILLING:

2 lb	tart apples, peeled, cored and sliced (6 to 8)	1 kg
3 tbsp	butter	45 mL
¼ cup	granulated sugar	50 mL
2 tbsp	lemon juice	25 mL
2 tbsp	Grand Marnier, orange liqueur or rum	25 mL

• Combine filling ingredients in saucepan. Simmer, covered, over medium heat until apples have exuded their juices, about 10 minutes. Continue to simmer, stirring occasionally, until juices have evaporated, about 15 minutes. Cool.
• Preheat oven to 350°F/180°C.
• Press half of dough into 9-inch/2.5-L springform pan to cover bottom and 2 inches/5 cm up sides. Spread filling on top of dough.
• Place remaining ball of dough on lightly floured board. Roll or press into 9-inch/23-cm circle. Carefully place on top of apple layer in pan. Press down lightly on edges to seal.
• Brush top of cake with beaten egg yolk. Trace lattice design over top using the prongs of a fork.
• Bake 50 minutes or until golden brown.

NOTE: This cake makes an excellent picnic or pot-luck party dessert, as it is easy to transport.

LEMON MAPLE TOFU CHEESECAKE

Karen Boulton perfected this unbeatable tofu cheesecake for the book I wrote with dietitian Rosie Schwartz called The Enlightened Eater. *It's as good as regular cheesecake, without the caloric side-effects.*

CRUST:

1½ cups	walnut pieces	375 mL
½ cup	quick-cooking (not instant) rolled oats	125 mL
3 tbsp	melted butter	45 mL
3 tbsp	maple syrup or liquid honey	45 mL

• Spread walnuts on cookie sheet in single layer. Toast in 400°F/200°C oven 5 minutes. Cool.

• Reduce oven temperature to 350°F/180°C.

• Place walnuts in food processor or blender with rolled oats. Process with a few on/off turns until coarsely chopped. Transfer mixture to bowl. Stir in melted butter and maple syrup. Pat into 9-inch/2.5-L springform pan. Bake 12 minutes. Cool.

FILLING:

1½ lb	tofu, well drained	750 g
2	eggs	2
	Grated rind and juice of 1 lemon	
½ cup	maple syrup or liquid honey	125 mL
1 tsp	grated peeled fresh ginger root	5 mL
pinch	salt	pinch

• Preheat oven to 350°F/180°C.

• Press tofu by wrapping in J-cloth and placing between two baking sheets with heavy weight (2 cans of food) on top for 30 minutes. Drain once or twice. Do not press more than 30 minutes. Blend in food processor until smooth. Add remaining ingredients. Process until smooth. Pour over cooled crust.

• Bake 50 minutes or until cake is set. Cool in pan.

ICING:

8 oz	tofu, drained	250 g
	Rind of 1 lemon	
	Juice of ½ lemon	
2 tbsp	maple syrup or liquid honey	25 mL
1 cup	blueberries, raspberries or strawberries	250 mL

- Puree all ingredients except berries in food processor.
- Remove rim of springform pan. Spread icing over cooled cake. Arrange berries attractively on top.

LINZERTORTE

My mother, Ruth Schachter, is one of the best bakers of European cakes and pastries. And I'm not biased! She has three recipes for linzertorte in her collection. This one is at the top of her list. Perfect with afternoon tea on a relaxed weekend, this cake appeared as part of "A Symphony of Sweets" in celebration of the 1985 movie hit, Amadeus. The secret is to use unpeeled almonds and top-notch raspberry jam. Homemade preserves (raspberry, plum or any dark fruit) work even better.

2 cups	whole almonds with skin on	500 mL
1 cup	unsalted butter (room temperature)	250 mL
1 cup	granulated sugar	250 mL
1	egg	1
1	egg yolk	1
	Grated rind and juice of ½ lemon	
1 tsp	grated orange rind	5 mL
½ tsp	ground cinnamon	2 mL
¼ tsp	ground allspice	1 mL
¼ tsp	ground cloves	1 mL
2 cups	all-purpose flour	500 mL
1 cup	good-quality raspberry, blackcurrant or plum jam	250 mL
1	egg white, lightly beaten	1
	Icing sugar for dusting	

- Grind almonds in food processor or blender until they resemble crumbs. Do not overprocess or they will turn into paste.
- Cream butter in bowl until light and smooth. Gradually beat in sugar until fluffy. Add egg, egg yolk, lemon juice and rinds. Beat well. Gradually stir in spices, flour and almonds. Gather dough into ball. Wrap in plastic wrap. Chill 1 hour.
- Preheat oven to 375°F/190°C.
- With floured hands, pat two-thirds of dough on bottom and part way up sides of 9-inch/23-cm flan ring with removable rim. Spread jam over dough.
- Roll out remaining dough on floured board until about ¼ inch/5 mm thick. Cut into strips ½ inch/1 cm wide. Arrange in lattice pattern on top of jam. Brush lattice top with beaten egg white.
- Bake 35 minutes or until golden brown. Cool in pan. Remove rim. Dust top with sifted icing sugar.

PLUM CAKE

The perfect use for the purple plums that are so plentiful in fall, this cakey tart from Kathleen Conway appeared in Open Kitchen in the fall of '85. Its understated elegance and delicate taste make it the perfect finale to a dinner party. Serve it with a little whipped cream, crème fraîche, vanilla ice cream or simply au naturel! Don't try to use canned plums in this—they are much too sweet.

CAKE:

½ cup	unsalted butter (room temperature)	125 mL
½ cup	granulated sugar	125 mL
2	eggs	2
1 cup	all-purpose flour, sifted	250 mL
1 tsp	baking powder	5 mL
pinch	salt	pinch
12 to 15	purple or red plums, pitted and halved	12 to 15

- Preheat oven to 350°F/180°C.
- Lightly butter 9-inch/2.5-L springform pan or flan ring with removable rim.
- Cream butter and sugar in bowl until light and creamy. Beat in eggs, one at a time, until fluffy. Stir in flour, baking powder and salt. Mix well. Turn into prepared pan and smooth top with knife.
- Place plums close together, skin side up, over entire surface of batter.

TOPPING:

2 tbsp	lemon juice	25 mL
2 tbsp	granulated sugar	25 mL
½ tsp	ground cinnamon	2 mL

- Sprinkle lemon juice evenly over plums. Then sprinkle over sugar and cinnamon.
- Bake 50 to 60 minutes or until golden brown. Cool.

ANDREA'S FUDGE CAKE

In the summer of '86, that excellent U.S. magazine, Chocolatier, *held a recipe contest. This was the winner. It came from Patricia Tyler, owner of the Belltown Cafe in Seattle, Washington, and would certainly have got my vote for chocolate decadence. Don't expect this cake to rise high when it comes out of the oven. It resembles a rich, giant brownie more than it does a cake. And I mean rich! Using a paper doily as a stencil when dusting the cake with icing sugar is Tyler's nifty idea for an elegant presentation.*

12 oz	semisweet chocolate, coarsely chopped	375 g
5 tbsp	instant espresso or instant coffee powder	75 mL
2 cups	granulated sugar	500 mL
1 cup	unsalted butter (room temperature)	250 mL
6	eggs, separated	6
1 cup	all-purpose flour	250 mL
	Icing sugar for dusting	

- Preheat oven to 350°F/180°C.
- Lightly butter and flour 9-inch/2.5-L springform pan.
- Melt chocolate and coffee in top of double boiler over barely simmering water. Remove from heat. Cool until lukewarm.
- Cream sugar and butter in large bowl or food processor until light and fluffy. Add egg yolks, one at a time, beating well after each addition. Stir in flour.
- Beat egg whites in separate bowl until stiff peaks form. Fold one-quarter of egg whites into melted chocolate. Then fold in remaining egg whites.
- Fold chocolate mixture into creamed mixture. Pour batter into prepared pan.
- Bake 60 to 70 minutes or until top is crusty and cracked and middle is still slightly moist. Cool in pan. Remove sides from pan. Transfer cake to serving plate. Place paper doily on top of cooled cake. Dust with icing sugar. Remove doily to reveal lacy design.

BLACK CAT HALLOWE'EN CAKE

A yummy Hallowe'en recipe from the people at Fry's Cocoa. This feline confection looks great, and how can it taste anything but superb with all that chocolate and peanut butter!

2 cups	all-purpose flour	500 mL
½ cup	unsweetened cocoa powder	125 mL
1 tbsp	baking powder	15 mL
¾ cup	butter (room temperature)	175 mL
½ cup	smooth peanut butter	125 mL
1½ cups	granulated sugar	375 mL
3	eggs	3
1½ tsp	vanilla	7 mL
1¾ cups	milk	425 mL

- Preheat oven to 350°F/180°C.
- Lightly butter two 9-inch/1.5-L round cake pans; line with wax paper.
- Sift together flour, cocoa and baking powder in bowl.
- Cream butter and peanut butter in large bowl until fluffy. Gradually beat in sugar. Add eggs, one at a time, beating well after each addition. Stir in vanilla.
- Add sifted dry ingredients to creamed mixture alternately with milk, mixing lightly after each addition. Divide batter between prepared pans.
- Bake 35 to 40 minutes or until toothpick comes out clean. Cool in pans 10 minutes. Remove from pans. Peel off wax paper. Cool completely on wire rack.

CHOCOLATE ICING:

⅓ cup	butter	75 mL
½ cup	unsweetened cocoa powder	125 mL
1 tsp	vanilla	5 mL
4 cups	sifted icing sugar	1 L
½ cup	milk	125 mL
	Colored candies (Smarties, gumdrops, etc.) for decorating	

- Melt butter in saucepan. Pour into large bowl. Stir in cocoa and vanilla. Alternately blend in icing sugar and milk until smooth and of spreading consistency.
- Place one cake layer on large tray for cat's body. Cut a circle about 6 inches/15 cm in diameter from second layer for cat's head, using a plate as guide.
- Place head above body on tray. Cut ears and tail from trimmings. Attach to cat's head with toothpicks. Spread icing evenly all over cat. Decorate with candies for eyes, nose, mouth and buttons.

DARK CHRISTMAS FRUITCAKE

Another recipe from my mother, Ruth Schachter, who recently gave me the most treasured of presents—a file folder containing her favorite recipes. Being a biologist, she has the scientific approach, combined with natural flair, that I think is needed to be a top-notch baker. This recipe for dark fruitcake is one of the best I've tried. Make it at least six weeks before Christmas. Wrap the cake in a J-cloth soaked in brandy or other booze; pour more booze on the cake at weekly intervals until ready to eat.

1 cup	butter (room temperature)	250 mL
1¾ cups	brown sugar	425 mL
1¾ cups	all-purpose flour, sifted	425 mL
1 tsp	each ground nutmeg, ginger, cloves and cinnamon	5 mL
2¾ cups	currants	675 mL
2¾ cups	sultanas	675 mL
¾ cup	raisins	175 mL
¾ cup	chopped glace cherries	175 mL
1 cup	mixed peel	250 mL
½ cup	ground almonds	125 mL
¼ cup	chopped walnuts	50 mL
3	eggs	3
¼ cup	brandy	50 mL
¼ cup	dry sherry	50 mL
	Grated rind and juice of 1 lemon and 1 orange	5 mL
1 tsp	rose water (optional)	5 mL
1 tsp	orange water (optional)	5 mL
2 tbsp	molasses	25 mL
2 tbsp	corn syrup	25 mL

• Preheat oven to 325°F/160°C.

• Lightly butter and flour 10-cup/2.5-L cake pan or mould. Set out three bowls—one very large and two large.

• Cream butter in very large bowl until fluffy. Gradually beat in sugar.

• Combine flour, spices, dried fruits and nuts in large bowl.

• Beat eggs, brandy, sherry, lemon rind and juice, orange rind and juice, rose water and orange water in remaining bowl.

• Heat molasses and corn syrup in small saucepan, stirring, until blended. Stir into egg mixture.

• Add fruit/flour mixture to creamed mixture alternately with egg mixture. Turn into prepared pan. Bake 1 hour. Reduce heat to 300°F/150°C. Continue baking 1 to 1½ hours or until toothpick inserted comes out clean. Time will vary depending on shape of pan. Cool in pan 10 minutes. Invert onto wire rack to cool completely. Store in airtight container.

CHOCOLATE CARROT CAKE

This runner-up in our 1987 Sweets for My Sweet Valentine's Contest was the creation of reader Mike Besser, who learned to experiment with baking when his family was in the restaurant business. From this luscious, moist cake with the nutrients of carrots and buttermilk, he obviously hasn't lost his knack.

3 oz	unsweetened chocolate	90 g
1⅓ cups	cake and pastry flour	325 mL
⅔ cup	cocoa powder	150 mL
1½ cups	granulated sugar	375 mL
1½ tsp	baking powder	7 mL
1½ tsp	baking soda	7 mL
½ tsp	salt	2 mL
2 tsp	ground cinnamon	10 mL
3	eggs	3
1 cup	vegetable oil	250 mL
2 tsp	vanilla	10 mL
1 tsp	lemon juice	5 mL
¾ cup	buttermilk	175 mL
2½ cups	grated carrots	625 mL
	Icing sugar for dusting	

- Preheat oven to 350°F/180°C.
- Lightly butter and flour 10-inch/3-L Bundt or tube pan.
- Melt chocolate in top of double boiler over barely simmering water. Cool to lukewarm.
- Combine flour, cocoa, sugar, baking powder, baking soda, salt and cinnamon in bowl. Mix well.
- Beat eggs in large bowl. Beat in oil, vanilla and lemon juice until light and creamy. Add buttermilk. Mix well.
- Stir flour mixture into egg mixture until combined. Stir in melted chocolate and carrots. Pour batter into prepared pan. Bake 50 minutes or until toothpick comes out clean. Cool in pan 15 minutes. Invert onto wire rack. Cool completely. Dust with sifted icing sugar just before serving.

DESSERTS

PECAN PIE

A superb recipe from Tom Hanes, chef and owner of Toronto Cajun restaurant, Tom and Jerry's. This is probably the most decadent thing ever to happen to a pecan.

1¾ cups	pecan halves	425 mL
¾ cup	Demerara sugar	175 mL
½ cup	corn syrup	125 mL
¼ cup	maple syrup	50 mL
¼ cup	melted butter	50 mL
3	eggs	3
½ tsp	all-purpose flour	2 mL
¼ tsp	ground nutmeg	1 mL
pinch	ground cloves	pinch
pinch	ground cinnamon	pinch
½ tsp	grated lemon rind	2 mL
1 tbsp	vanilla	15 mL
2 tbsp	bourbon, rum or whisky	25 mL
1	9-inch/23-cm unbaked pie shell	1
	Whipped cream for garnish	
	Ground cinnamon for garnish	

- Preheat oven to 350°F/180°C.
- Spread pecans on baking sheet. Toast in oven 5 minutes or until aromatic. Cool.
- Whisk remaining ingredients except garnishes in bowl.
- Spread pecans in pie shell. Pour in filling. Bake 35 to 40 minutes or until sides are firm and middle is slightly soft. If pie puffs up, prick with fork. Cool at least 30 minutes. Serve warm or at room temperature. Top with whipped cream and cinnamon.

LEMON HEAVEN PIE

The idea for this pie came from André Théberge at The Parrot restaurant on Queen Street in Toronto. We adapted it to combine a tantalizing, crisp gingersnap crust with a mile-high fluffy filling that will send your tastebuds to Cloud Nine. To make crumbs, process gingersnap cookies briefly in food processor or crush with rolling pin.

CRUST:

1¼ cups	gingersnap cookie crumbs	300 mL
⅓ cup	melted butter	75 mL

- Preheat oven to 350°F/180°C.
- Combine cookie crumbs and butter in bowl. Press into 9-inch/23-cm pie plate. Bake 15 minutes. Cool.

FILLING:

3	eggs, separated, plus 1 extra egg white	3
¼ cup	dry white wine	50 mL
1 tsp	unflavored gelatin	5 mL
	Grated rind of 1 lemon	
⅓ cup	lemon juice (about 1½ lemons)	75 mL
½ cup	granulated sugar	125 mL
1 cup	whipping cream	250 mL

- Add yolks, wine, gelatin, lemon rind, juice and ¼ cup/50 mL sugar to top of double boiler. Whisk constantly over simmering water until thickened, about 5 minutes. Cool to room temperature. Do not refrigerate.
- In separate bowl, beat egg whites until stiff. Gradually add remaining sugar, beating well after each addition.
- Beat whipping cream in another bowl until soft peaks form. Gently fold into lemon mixture. Fold in whites. Pile into pie shell. Refrigerate 3 to 4 hours, or until firm.

SOUR CREAM APPLE PIE

A delectable down-home variation on that all-American theme from food writer, Carol White. I'll bet even Grandma's didn't taste this good! Use a tart apple but not the Granny Smith variety, since they refuse to soften when cooked.

1	9-inch/23-cm unbaked deep-dish pie shell	1
2 tbsp	all-purpose flour	25 mL
6 to 8	tart apples, peeled, cored and thinly sliced	6 to 8
1 tbsp	cold butter, cut in pieces	15 mL
1½ cups	sour cream	375 mL
¾ cup	brown sugar	175 mL
3	egg yolks, lightly beaten	3

- Preheat oven to 425°F/220°C.
- Sprinkle pie shell with 1 tbsp/15 mL flour. Arrange apple slices in shell. Dot with butter. Sprinkle remaining flour on top.
- Combine sour cream, brown sugar and egg yolks in bowl. Pour or spoon over apples. Bake 15 minutes. Reduce heat to 350°F/180°C. Bake 40 minutes or until apples are tender. Serve warm or at room temperature.

Pear Almond Tart

One of the best desserts I've ever tasted, this was the winner of Open Kitchen's "Parlez-Vous Gourmet" Contest, in which readers submitted favorite French recipes. Robin Tucker came up with this idea after a trip to France. She recreated what she'd tasted by consulting cookbooks and adding her own touches. Be careful when selecting the pears. They must be ripe or they won't cook through. Bosc or Anjou varieties are best for taste and texture.

CRUST:

1 cup	cake and pastry flour	250 mL
¼ cup	icing sugar	50 mL
½ cup	cold butter	125 mL
1	egg	1
1 tsp	vanilla	5 mL

• Sift together flour and icing sugar. Cut in butter with two knives or pastry cutter until mixture resembles coarse crumbs.

• Beat egg and vanilla together in separate bowl. Add one-third of egg mixture to flour mixture. Mix with fork until dough forms ball, adding remaining egg mixture as required.

• Roll out dough on floured surface or pat into 9-inch/23-cm pie plate or flan ring with removable rim. Chill 30 minutes.

FILLING:

4	ripe pears, peeled, cored and halved	4
½ cup	butter (room temperature)	125 mL
½ cup	granulated sugar	125 mL
1 cup	ground almonds	250 mL
2	eggs	2
1 tsp	vanilla	5 mL
1 tsp	almond extract	5 mL
⅓ cup	sliced almonds	75 mL

• Preheat oven to 375°F/190°C. Drain pears on paper towels.

• Cream butter until light. Add sugar, ground almonds, eggs, vanilla and almond extract. Beat until fluffy. Turn into pie shell. Place 7 pear halves in circle; place remaining half in centre. Bake 20 minutes.

• Reduce heat to 350°F/180°C and bake 20 minutes more. Sprinkle almonds on tart and bake 20 minutes or until golden brown. Cool 20 minutes.

GLAZE:

½ cup	apricot jam	125 mL
2 tbsp	water	25 mL

• Melt jam with water in small saucepan. Strain through sieve. Brush glaze over tart.

PEANUT BUTTER PIE

Words can hardly describe the taste and texture of this pie. Sinfully rich when ungarnished, it is wickedly wonderful served with warm fudge sauce. This creation comes from Greg Downie, who was chef at the Grey Goat in Newmarket, Ontario, when his recipe appeared in the Sun.

CRUST:

1 cup	pecans	250 mL
¼ cup	icing sugar, sifted	50 mL
¼ cup	melted butter	50 mL
½ cup	Graham cracker crumbs	125 mL

• Toast pecans in heavy skillet over low heat, shaking constantly, about 5 minutes or until aromatic. Cool. Grind in food processor or blender until the texture of coarse crumbs. Don't overprocess. Combine with icing sugar, butter and cracker crumbs in bowl. Pat into 9-inch/23-cm pie pan. Chill at least 30 minutes.

FILLING:

1¼ cups	good-quality peanut butter (smooth or crunchy)	300 mL
1¼ cups	icing sugar, sifted	300 mL
8 oz	soft deli cream cheese (room temperature)	250 g
1 tsp	vanilla	5 mL
1¼ cups	whipping cream	300 mL

• Combine all ingredients except cream in bowl. Mix well.
• Whip cream to soft peaks in small bowl. Fold into peanut butter mixture. Turn into pie shell. Refrigerate at least 1 hour.

FUDGE SAUCE:

6 oz	semisweet chocolate chips	175 g
¼ cup	unsalted butter	50 mL
2 tbsp	strong coffee	25 mL
¼ cup	whipping cream	50 mL

• Melt chocolate and butter in saucepan over low heat, stirring. Stir in coffee and cream.

Makes about 1 cup.

CRÈME FRAÎCHE BERRY TART

This creation, by inspired chef Jonn (pronounced Joan) Richardson, is worth every ounce of effort and every calorie. The crème fraîche layer that goes between the crust and fruit is a wonderful original touch. Jonn used blackberries for her version. Raspberries, strawberries or blueberries would also work well.

CRÈME FRAÎCHE:

2 cups	whipping cream	500 mL
½ cup	granulated sugar	125 mL
½ tsp	vanilla	2 mL
2 tbsp	sour cream	25 mL
	Juice of ½ lemon	

• Whisk together all ingredients in bowl. Cover with plastic wrap. Let sit at room temperature 3 days. Line sieve with cheesecloth, J-cloth or paper towel. Pour in crème fraîche and set over bowl to drain in fridge 4 to 6 hours. Discard watery liquid that collects in bowl. Crème fraîche will be consistency of thick sour cream.

CRUST:

1½ cups	pecans or walnuts	375 mL
⅓ cup	icing sugar, sifted	75 mL
⅓ cup	melted butter	75 mL
¾ cup	Graham cracker crumbs	175 mL

• Shaking constantly, toast nuts in heavy skillet over low heat until aromatic, about 5 minutes. Cool. Grind in food processor or blender until they resemble coarse crumbs. Don't overprocess. Combine with icing sugar, butter and cracker crumbs in bowl. Mix well. Pat into 9-inch/23-cm flan ring with removable rim, or pie plate. Chill.

TOPPING:

2 cups	fresh berries	500 mL
⅓ cup	apricot jam or red current jelly	75 mL
2 tbsp	water	25 mL

• Fill pie shell with crème fraîche. Arrange berries attractively on top, starting at outer edge and working in.
• Melt jam with water in small saucepan. Strain through sieve. Brush over fruit. Chill.

LEMON RASPBERRY PARFAIT

An elegant fruit ice cream that looks as gorgeous as it tastes, created by Joanne Yolles of Scaramouche restaurant in Toronto. This recipe appeared in an article called "Sweet Dreams," in which four Toronto pastry chefs were photographed in the land of slumber, where desserts like this are sweet reverie. The parfait has two gorgeously contrasting colored layers and can be made in a springform pan with removable rim or in a fancy mould.

RASPBERRY SAUCE:

2	300-g packages unsweetened frozen raspberries, thawed	2
¼ cup	granulated sugar or to taste	50 mL
1 tbsp	lemon juice or to taste	15 mL

- Puree raspberries in food processor or blender until smooth. Strain through sieve to remove seeds. Add sugar and lemon juice. Stir to combine.

¾ cup	granulated sugar	175 mL
	Grated rind of 1½ lemons	
¼ cup	lemon juice (1 small lemon)	50 mL
4	eggs, separated, yolks divided between two bowls	4
1½ cups	whipping cream	375 mL
	Fresh raspberries for garnish (optional)	

- Add 2 tbsp/25 mL sugar, lemon rind and juice to two egg yolks in one of the two bowls. Place bowl over saucepan of barely simmering water. Whisk constantly until mixture thickens, about 5 minutes. Cool.
- Add ½ cup/125 mL raspberry sauce and 1 tbsp/15 mL sugar to second bowl of egg yolks. Set bowl over saucepan of barely simmering water. Whisk constantly until mixture thickens, about 5 minutes. Cool.
- Beat egg whites in separate bowl until foamy. Add remaining sugar, 1 tbsp/15 mL at a time, beating until whites are stiff but not dry.
- Beat cream in separate bowl until soft peaks form.
- Fold half of beaten egg whites and half of whipped cream into lemon mixture.
- Fold remaining egg whites and whipped cream into raspberry mixture.
- Turn lemon mixture into 8-inch/2-L springform pan. Smooth top with knife. Top with raspberry mixture. Smooth top with knife. Cover with plastic wrap. Freeze at least 6 hours or overnight.
- Remove from springform pan and pour remaining raspberry sauce on parfait to serve. Garnish with raspberries.

Serves 6 to 8.

BONNIE'S RICE PUDDING

This comfort food classic comes from Bonnie Stern's cookbook, At My Table, *and is tops in its genre.*

½ cup	short-grain rice	125 mL
1 cup	boiling water	250 mL
5 cups	milk	1.25 L
⅓ cup	granulated sugar	75 mL
1 tsp	cornstarch	5 mL
½ cup	raisins	125 mL
pinch	salt	pinch
pinch	ground nutmeg	pinch
2	egg yolks, beaten	2
1 tsp	vanilla	5 mL
	Ground cinnamon for garnish	

• Combine rice and boiling water in heavy saucepan. Cover; simmer 15 minutes or until all water is absorbed. Stir all but ½ cup/125 mL milk into rice, slowly bringing mixture to boil.

• Combine sugar, cornstarch and remaining ½ cup/125 mL milk in small bowl. Stir until smooth. Add to rice mixture. Add raisins, salt and nutmeg. When mixture comes to boil, reduce heat to low. Cover; simmer until rice is thick and creamy, stirring occasionally. Patience is required at this point; it takes about 2 hours for pudding to thicken.

• When thickened, add some pudding to egg yolks in bowl. Return egg mixture to pudding. Cook over low heat 1 minute. Stir in vanilla. Spoon into dessert dishes or one large bowl. Sprinkle generously with cinnamon. Serve with cream on side.

Serves 8.

CHOCOLATE MOUSSE

One of my all-time favorite recipes, this easy, melt-in-the-mouth mousse from my caterer friend Sassy Waddell is one of the less caloric versions I have found. It is also the tastiest.

12 oz	bittersweet chocolate, cut in small chunks, or semisweet chocolate chips	375 g
¾ cup	very hot double-strength black coffee	175 mL
6	eggs, separated	6
2 to 3 tbsp	brandy, Scotch or dark rum	25 to 45 mL

- Place chocolate in blender or food processor. Pour in coffee. Blend until chocolate melts and mixture is smooth. Blend in egg yolks, one at a time. Blend in brandy. Transfer to bowl.
- Beat egg whites in separate bowl until soft peaks form. Fold gently into chocolate mixture until no white shows. Chill in individual dessert glasses (wine glasses work well) or one large glass dish.

Serves 6.

MUD PIE

Kids of all ages adore this frozen chocolate creation from Hughie's restaurant on Front Street in Toronto. Absolutely delicious and a cinch to make, it is best eaten in small amounts.

20	Oreo cookies	20
¼ cup	melted unsalted butter	50 mL
4 cups	coffee-flavored ice cream, slightly softened	1 L
4 tsp	coffee liqueur or water	20 mL
2 tbsp	corn syrup	25 mL
4 tsp	unsalted butter, cut in pieces	20 mL
2 oz	semisweet chocolate, coarsely chopped	60 g
1 oz	unsweetened chocolate, coarsely chopped	30 g
½ cup	whipping cream	125 mL
¼ tsp	vanilla	1 mL
½ tsp	icing sugar	2 mL
	Grated semisweet chocolate for garnish	

- Grind cookies and melted butter in food processor or blender until they resemble coarse crumbs.
- Line 9-inch/23-cm pie plate with foil. Press crumbs into pie plate with back of spoon. Freeze 30 minutes. Peel foil off crust; place crust back in pie plate. (This step prevents crust from sticking to pie plate when serving.)
- Spoon ice cream into crust. Return to freezer 1 hour.
- Bring liqueur, corn syrup and butter to boil in small saucepan. Remove from heat. Whisk in chocolate until melted and smooth. Cool. Pour glaze over ice cream. Spread with knife, working quickly before glaze hardens. Return to freezer until ready to serve.
- Just before serving, whip cream, vanilla and icing sugar together in bowl until soft peaks form. Mound onto pie. Sprinkle with grated chocolate.

BREAD PUDDING WITH BOURBON SAUCE

With the return of down-home cooking, bread pudding is making a well-deserved comeback and is now being served in many a fancy restaurant. This version, from the now-defunct Stage Door Cafe in Toronto, was created by chef André Valiquette and is simply out of this world. The bourbon sauce is great with it, but you could substitute ice cream or your favorite custard. This makes a large pudding; cut recipe in half if desired.

PUDDING:

½	large loaf French bread torn in pieces (about 10 cups/2.5 L)	½
½ cup	milk	125 mL
3 cups	light cream	750 mL
6	eggs, separated	6
1½ cups	granulated sugar	375 mL
	Grated rind and juice of 1 lemon	
2 tsp	vanilla	10 mL
1 tsp	ground cinnamon	5 mL
1 tsp	ground nutmeg	5 mL
1 cup	raisins	250 mL

- Preheat oven to 350°F/180°C.
- Butter 8-cup/2-L ovenproof dish. Place bread in dish.
- Whisk together milk, cream, egg yolks, 1¼ cups/300 mL sugar, lemon rind, lemon juice, vanilla, cinnamon and nutmeg in large bowl. Stir in raisins. Pour mixture over bread.
- Bake 15 minutes; stir, then bake 15 minutes more.
- Remove from oven. Cool to room temperature. Stir pudding to break up bread and make pudding smoother.
- Beat egg whites until foamy. Gradually beat in remaining ¼ cup/ 50 mL sugar until soft peaks form. Fold into pudding. Return to oven. Bake 25 minutes or until top is golden brown. Serve with bourbon sauce (below):

BOURBON SAUCE:

¼ cup	granulated sugar	50 mL
1 cup	light cream	250 mL
2	egg yolks	2
2 tbsp	bourbon, dark rum or whisky	25 mL
	Fresh berries in season for garnish	
	Fresh mint leaves for garnish (optional)	

• Whisk together sugar, cream, egg yolks and bourbon in top of double boiler. Stir constantly over simmering water until sauce thickens, 5 to 7 minutes.

• Garnish pudding with berries and mint. Serve hot bourbon sauce on the side.

Serves 8 to 10.

GRANOLA FRUIT CRUMBLE

Granola gives extra crunch to this super topping. Use the type without raisins — they will burn. Rhubarb is one of my favorite fruits in crumble, and it works well in combination with apples or strawberries. If using rhubarb, alone or with other fruit, toss with about ½ cup/125 mL sugar to combat tartness.

Use frozen fruit if making this in winter. You can peel fruit like apples or pears, though I prefer not to, both for flavor and the nutritional bonus of added fibre.

5 to 6 cups	sliced fruit	1.25 to 1.5 L
1 tsp	ground cinnamon	5 mL

• Preheat oven to 350°F/180°C. Lightly butter a 13 × 9-inch/3.5-L ovenproof dish.

• Toss fruit with cinnamon in bowl. (If using rhubarb, add ½ cup/ 125 mL sugar at this point.) Turn into prepared dish.

	TOPPING:	
½ cup	all-purpose flour	125 mL
¾ cup	granola (without raisins) or quick-cooking (not instant) rolled oats	175 mL
½ cup	brown sugar	125 mL
½ cup	butter	125 mL

• Combine flour, granola and brown sugar in bowl. Cut butter into dry ingredients, using two knives or pastry blender, until crumbly. Sprinkle on fruit.

• Bake 45 to 50 minutes or until bubbly and fruit is tender. Serve with vanilla ice cream, crème fraîche (see page 164) or sweetened yogurt.

Serves 6 to 8.

BLUEBERRY PEACH CRUMBLE

This easy-to-make crumble is the invention of Dinah Koo, well-known Toronto caterer and owner of Dinah's Cupboard. Originally designed for the microwave, this dish is also excellent cooked the conventional way. Use whatever fresh fruits and berries are in season. The blueberry/peach combination is yummy and a terrific seasonal match.

2 tbsp	all-purpose flour	25 mL
½ cup	brown sugar	125 mL
2 tbsp	ground cinnamon	25 mL
6 cups	sliced fresh peaches	1.5 L
2 cups	blueberries	500 mL

• Combine flour, sugar and cinnamon in large bowl. Toss in fruit. Place in 13 × 9-inch/3.5-L buttered ovenproof dish.

TOPPING:

½ cup	sliced almonds	125 mL
1 cup	raw rolled oats (not quick-cooking)	250 mL
1 tbsp	ground cinnamon	15 mL
¼ cup	brown sugar	50 mL
¼ cup	butter (room temperature)	50 mL

• Preheat oven to 425°F/220°C.
• Shaking constantly, toast almonds in heavy skillet over low heat until golden brown. Cool. Combine with remaining topping ingredients in bowl. Sprinkle over fruit.
• Bake 20 to 30 minutes or until edges bubble. Serve with vanilla ice cream or whipped cream.

Serves 8.

MAPLE CARAMEL APPLES

Another recipe from Sun *recipe cartoonist, Frances Beaulieu. These should keep those little witches and goblins happy on Hallowe'en. A great party idea, whatever the occasion.*

1½ cups	dark brown sugar	375 mL
1½ cups	maple syrup	375 mL
½ cup	whipping cream	125 mL
1 tbsp	butter	15 mL
10 to 12	apples	10 to 12
10 to 12	wooden skewers	10 to 12

- Combine brown sugar, maple sugar and cream in large heavy saucepan. Cook over medium heat, stirring constantly; brush crystals that cling to sides of saucepan into sugar mixture with pastry brush dipped in cold water. Bring syrup to boil. Cook to firm ball stage (248°F/120°C), i.e., when syrup dropped into cold water forms a firm ball which does not flatten on removal from water.
- Remove syrup from heat. Add butter. Swirl pan until butter melts. Cool 5 minutes.
- Place one apple on each skewer. Dip apples, one at a time, into caramel, letting excess drip off. Let sit on buttered cookie sheet until hardened.

Makes 10 to 12.

WINTER FRUIT COMPOTE

Fruit salad can be just as tasty in winter as it is in summer. I like this version, made with prunes and any other dried fruit you'd like to use (apricots and figs work well), just as much as the fresh fruit variety. I offered this as a breakfast idea in the winter of '87, but it is delicious at any time of day.

½ cup	unsweetened apple juice	125 mL
1	cinnamon stick	1
2	cloves	2
⅓ cup	pitted prunes, halved	75 mL
¼ cup	orange juice	50 mL
1	tart apple, cored and thinly sliced	1
1	ripe pear, peeled, cored and sliced	1
1 cup	seedless green grapes, halved	250 mL
2	navel oranges, peeled and sectioned	2

- Combine apple juice, cinnamon stick and cloves in small saucepan. Bring to boil; reduce heat. Simmer, uncovered, 10 minutes. Remove from heat. Stir in prunes and orange juice. Let sit 10 minutes or until prunes are soft. Transfer mixture to bowl. Cool. Remove cinnamon stick and cloves. Stir in fruit. Refrigerate, covered, at least 2 hours.

Serves 4.

TIRAMISU

"Sinfully rich" is an understatement when it comes to describing this dessert! As common on Italian restaurant menus as apple pie is on this continent, tiramisu should come with a warning: Only eat a small portion and invite lots of friends over to finish the rest! This recipe was inspired by my visit to Italy in the fall of '86.

1 lb	soft deli cream cheese	500 g
½ cup	icing sugar	125 mL
½ cup	Kahlua or other coffee-flavored liqueur	125 mL
1 tsp	vanilla	5 mL
3 oz	good-quality bittersweet chocolate, coarsely grated	90 g
1½ cups	whipping cream	375 mL
2 tsp	instant espresso or regular instant coffee powder	10 mL
2 tbsp	water	25 mL
16	ladyfinger biscuits, cut in half lengthwise	16

• Beat cream cheese, icing sugar, ¼ cup/50 mL Kahlua and vanilla in food processor or bowl until light and fluffy. Stir in 2 oz/60 g grated chocolate.

• Whip 1 cup/250 mL cream in separate bowl until soft peaks form. Fold into cheese mixture.

• Combine coffee powder, remaining Kahlua and water in another small bowl.

• Line large decorative glass bowl or rectangular dish with 8 ladyfinger slices. Brush with coffee mixture. Spread layer of cream cheese mixture on top. Repeat layers, finishing with cream cheese mixture.

• In small bowl, whip remaining cream until soft peaks form. Garnish dessert with whipped cream and remaining grated chocolate. Cover and chill at least 2 hours.

Serves 12 to 16.

NOTE: For an even more elegant presentation, line bowl with plastic wrap before layering dessert on top. To serve, invert onto plate after chilling and garnish with whipped cream and grated chocolate.

MANGO MOUSSE

"It Takes Two to Mango" was my eulogy to this most wonderful of tropical fruits in fall, 1986. In many places you can find mangoes during most of the year; what better way to use them than in this light-as-air mousse.

2	large mangoes, peeled, pitted and coarsely chopped	2
⅓ cup	fresh lime or lemon juice	75 mL
2	egg whites	2
¼ cup	granulated sugar	50 mL
½ cup	whipping cream	125 mL

• Blend mango and lime juice in food processor or blender until blended but not completely smooth. Transfer to medium bowl.

• Beat egg whites in separate bowl until soft peaks form. Beat in 1 tbsp/ 15 mL sugar at a time until stiff, but not dry, peaks form.

• In separate bowl, beat cream until soft peaks form; fold into mango mixture. Gently fold in beaten egg white mixture. Spoon into dessert cups or wine glasses. Refrigerate at least 4 hours.

Serves 4 to 6.

SATIN SAUCE 'N' STRAWBERRIES

The clever people at Foodland Ontario came up with this incredible silken sauce that's perfect for smothering on fresh home-grown strawberries.

1	egg	1
2	egg yolks	2
⅓ cup	granulated sugar	75 mL
¼ tsp	salt	1 mL
1 tsp	lemon juice	5 mL
1 cup	unflavored yogurt	250 mL
¾ cup	whipping cream	175 mL
1 tsp	vanilla	5 mL
10 cups	fresh strawberries	2.5 L

• Whisk egg, yolks, sugar and salt in top of double boiler until blended. Set over simmering water; cook, whisking constantly, until thickened, 5 to 7 minutes. Stir in lemon juice. Cool to room temperature. Whisk in yogurt.

• Combine cream and vanilla in medium bowl. Beat until soft peaks form. Fold into yogurt mixture. Chill. Whisk again just before serving if sauce separates. Serve over whole or sliced berries.

Makes about 2½ cups/625 mL. Serves 8 to 10.

CHOCOLATE-DIPPED STRAWBERRIES

Strawberries are my favorite fruit to use in this recipe that was featured in a 1987 Valentine's Day article called "Feeding Bawdy and Soul." What could be more romantic than nibbling on a few of these while sipping Champagne or coffee with brandy after a romantic dinner à deux. Work quickly, so the chocolate doesn't cool and harden. If it does, just return it to heat until it melts again.

6 oz	good-quality semisweet chocolate, chopped	175 g
2 cups	fresh strawberries, unhulled	500 mL

• Melt chocolate in top of double boiler over barely simmering water, stirring occasionally. Remove from heat.
• Dip strawberries into melted chocolate to coat tip and about three-quarters of way up. Place on wax paper. cool. Refrigerate, uncovered, until chocolate is firm.

PUMPKIN MERINGUE PIE

A new twist to the classic theme, this makes a terrific change for Thanksgiving dinner. The meringue topping also does visual wonders for this usually ho-hum-looking dessert. When separating the eggs to make the filling, reserve the egg whites for the meringue.

1	9-inch/23-cm unbaked pie shell	1
	FILLING:	
1	14-oz/398-mL can pumpkin puree	1
½ cup	granulated sugar	125 mL
1 tsp	ground cinnamon	5 mL
¼ tsp	ground nutmeg	1 mL
¼ tsp	ground cloves	1 mL
3	egg yolks	3
1 cup	evaporated milk	250 mL

• Preheat oven to 400°F/200°C.
• Combine pumpkin puree, sugar and spices in bowl. Mix well. Add egg yolks. Blend well. Gradually stir in evaporated milk. Pour into pie shell. Bake 35 minutes or until toothpick inserted comes out clean. Remove pie from oven.
• Increase oven temperature to 425°F/220°C.

MERINGUE:

3	egg whites	3	
pinch	salt	pinch	
⅓ cup	granulated sugar	75 mL	

- Beat egg whites and salt in bowl until foamy. Gradually beat in sugar until stiff peaks form. Spread meringue on pie, starting at crust edge and heaping it higher in centre. Bake 5 minutes or until meringue is lightly browned. Cool on rack.

APPLE FRITTERS

Jacques Pépin, French chef and cooking pro living in New England, demonstrated this marvellous dessert at a cooking class he gave in Toronto at the Bonnie Stern School of Cooking in 1984. Beer makes the batter unbelievably light and crisp. Use tart apples and a good-quality oil such as sunflower, safflower or peanut.

1	355-mL can beer	1
1½ cups	all-purpose flour	375 mL
2 lb	apples (6 to 8 medium)	1 kg
	Vegetable oil for deep-frying	
	Icing sugar for dusting	

- Combine two-thirds of beer and all of flour in bowl. Mix together with whisk until smooth. Whisk in remaining beer. Batter should be consistency of thick, heavy syrup. Let sit at room temperature 1 hour.
- Peel and core apples. Cut in slices between ¼ inch/5 mm and ½ inch/ 1 cm thick. Stack slices on top of one another. Cut into sticks about ¼ inch/ 5 mm wide. Add to batter.
- Add oil to skillet to depth of 2 inches/5 cm. Heat oil to 350°F/180°C.
- Gently slide 2 to 3 tbsp/25 to 45 mL mixture into hot oil. Cook only a few fritters at a time, being careful not to crowd pan. Cook about 1½ minutes per side or until golden brown all over. Remove from oil with slotted spoon. Drain in paper towels. Dust with sifted icing sugar.

Serves 6 to 8.

CHRISTMAS PUDDING

My mother has been making this beer-laced Christmas pud for many moons. Only recently did I discover that her recipe comes from Guinness breweries. The results are superb. This pudding keeps almost indefinitely; I recently served one that had been sitting wrapped in foil in a cool cupboard for three years. I began dousing it in brandy and Scotch about three months before we ate it smothered in custard. And was it good!

5 cups	fresh breadcrumbs	1.25 L
1¾ cups	brown sugar	425 mL
1 tsp	salt	5 mL
2 tsp	allspice	10 mL
1¾ cups	currants	425 mL
2 cups	raisins	500 mL
1½ cups	sultanas	375 mL
10 oz	beef suet	300 g
½ cup	chopped mixed peel	125 mL
2	eggs, beaten	2
	Grated rind of 1 lemon	
1 tbsp	lemon juice	15 mL
⅔ cup	milk	150 mL
1¼ cups	Guinness or other stout beer	300 mL

• Combine breadcrumbs, brown sugar, salt, allspice, currants, raisins, sultanas, suet and mixed peel in large bowl. Mix well.

• Combine remaining ingredients in separate bowl. Add to dry ingredients. Mix well. Turn batter into two 4-cup/1-L moulds. Press down with back of spoon. Tie cheesecloth, J-cloth or foil around each mould, sealing well. Refrigerate overnight or longer. Or store wrapped in foil or brandy-soaked J-cloth in cool place.

• Steam puddings 4 hours. If not eating immediately, cool, re-wrap, store in cool place or freeze and then steam 2 to 3 hours before serving. Serve with hard sauce or custard.

Serves 8 to 10.

JELLY HOLLY WREATH

A gorgeous creation from cooking teacher Temi Rosenthal that is the ideal solution for those little people who don't enjoy the traditional pudding for Christmas dessert. It will also be a hit at any kids' party. Those spearmint leaves found at some candy counters are perfect as holly leaves. The kids will love to help decorate, so let them in on the fun.

1	85-g package lemon gelatin	1
	Red and green gumdrops or jelly beans, cut in half lengthwise	
1	85-g package strawberry gelatin	1
1 cup	sour cream or unflavored yogurt	250 mL
8	green maraschino cherries, chopped	8
½ cup	chopped walnuts	125 mL
1	85-g package lime gelatin	1
8	red maraschino cherries, chopped	8
1	85-g package raspberry gelatin	1

• Dissolve lemon gelatin in 1 cup/250 mL boiling water. Add ¾ cup/175 mL cold water. Stir until blended. Spoon some of mixture into 10-cup/2.5-L ring mould or Bundt pan in layer about ¼ inch/5 mm thick. Refrigerate until partially set, about 30 minutes. Arrange green and red gumdrops in gelatin layer to resemble holly wreath and berries. Refrigerate until set. Spoon on remaining lemon gelatin. Refrigerate until set, about 1 hour.

• Dissolve strawberry gelatin in 1 cup/250 mL boiling water. Add ¾ cup/175 mL cold water and ⅓ cup/75 mL sour cream. Stir until blended. Refrigerate until partially set. Stir in green cherries and half of nuts. Spoon over lemon layer. Refrigerate until set, about 1 hour.

• Dissolve lime gelatin in 1 cup/250 mL boiling water. Add ¾ cup/175 mL cold water and ⅓ cup/75 mL sour cream. Stir until blended. Refrigerate until partially set. Stir in red cherries and remaining nuts. Spoon over strawberry layer. Refrigerate until set, about 1 hour.

• Dissolve raspberry gelatin in 1 cup/250 mL boiling water. Add ¾ cup/175 mL cold water and remaining sour cream. Stir until blended. Refrigerate until partially set. Spoon over lime layer. Refrigerate until set, about 1 hour.

• To unmould, dip mould in sinkful of hot water for a few seconds. Invert onto large plate. Garnish with red and green gumdrops if desired.

Serves 14 to 16.

FROZEN PUMPKIN CRUMBLE

From Sun *columnist Karen Boulton, this mouth-watering pumpkin recipe has long been a Thanksgiving tradition in her family as a refreshing alternative to pie at the end of a filling meal. It's also much simpler to make.*

CRUST:

1½ cups	Graham cracker crumbs	375 mL
¼ cup	granulated sugar	50 mL
½ cup	butter, melted	125 mL

- Preheat oven to 375°F/190°C.
- Combine crumbs, sugar and butter in bowl. Mix well. Set aside ¼ cup/50 mL for topping. Pat remaining mixture into 9-inch/23-cm round pie pan or ovenproof dish. Bake 10 minutes. Cool.

FILLING:

1	14-oz/398-mL can pumpkin puree or 1¾ cups/425 mL homemade	1
2 cups	ice cream (vanilla, butter pecan or maple walnut), softened	500 mL
¼ tsp	ground nutmeg	1 mL
½ tsp	ground cinnamon	2 mL
½ tsp	ground ginger	2 mL
¼ tsp	salt	1 mL

- Mix together all filling ingredients in bowl with fork or large spoon. Turn into cooled pie shell; smooth top with knife. Sprinkle reserved crumb mixture on top. Freeze until firm, at least 2 hours. Remove from freezer about 15 minutes before serving.

Serves 6 to 8.

POTPOURRI

PICCALILLI

Helen Pennington, wife of Sun *entertainment columnist, Bob Pennington, betrays her English roots with this recipe that was a popular item in Open Kitchen. A sweet-and-sour condiment, it goes well with cold meat or cheese.*

1 cup	coarse pickling salt	250 mL
8 cups	cold water	2 L
1	small cauliflower, cut in small pieces	1
1 lb	small pearl onions, blanched and skin removed	500 g
1	medium onion, chopped	1
1	unpeeled English cucumber, diced	1
2	underripe tomatoes, diced	2
12 oz	green beans, topped, tailed and cut in 1-inch/2-cm pieces (about 2 cups/500 mL)	375 g
⅓ cup	all-purpose flour	75 mL
4 tsp	dry mustard	20 mL
2 tsp	ground turmeric	10 mL
4 cups	malt vinegar	1 L
¼ cup	granulated sugar	50 mL

• Combine salt and water in large bowl; stir until salt is dissolved. Add vegetables. Cover; chill 24 hours. Drain brine from vegetables. Discard brine.

• Combine flour, mustard and turmeric in small bowl. Add ½ cup/125 mL vinegar. Whisk together to form smooth paste. Transfer mixture to large saucepan. Slowly stir in remaining vinegar. Bring mixture to boil, stirring constantly. Add sugar and vegetables. Bring to boil; reduce heat. Simmer, uncovered, 5 minutes.

• Spoon piccalilli into sterilized jars.

Makes about 12 cups/3 L.

NOTE: This is ready to serve 24 hours after being cooked.

MANGO SAUCE

An idea that came to me one day when I was barbecuing chicken and felt the need for sauce. Mangoes have enough juice and flavor to make them perfect candidates for this. You can thin the puree out with white wine instead of chicken stock or yogurt. Use whipping cream instead of yogurt if calories are of no concern.

1	large ripe mango, peeled, pitted and coarsely chopped	1
¼ cup	chicken stock	50 mL
¼ cup	unflavored yogurt	50 mL

• Puree all ingredients in food processor or blender until smooth. Heat if serving warm, just until heated through. Do not boil. Or serve cold.

Serves 4 to 6 as sauce to accompany meat, poultry or fish. Makes about 1 cup.

MANGO CHUTNEY

Food consultant Sheila Swerling-Puritt is the brains behind this top-notch prescription for a condiment that's a must to go with any East Indian meal. It was part of an article called "It Takes Two to Mango."

6 to 7	medium ripe mangoes, peeled, pitted and sliced (about 3½ cups/875 mL)	6 to 7
2½ cups	granulated sugar	625 mL
1 cup	brown sugar	250 mL
1 cup	cider vinegar	250 mL
4	cloves garlic, minced	4
¼ cup	finely chopped fresh ginger root	50 mL
1½ tsp	salt	7 mL
1 tsp	chili powder	5 mL
1½ tsp	whole cloves, tied up in cheesecloth bag	7 mL
½ cup	raisins	125 mL
½ cup	sultanas	125 mL

• Combine mangoes and sugars in bowl. Let sit in fridge overnight. Drain mangoes, reserving syrup.

• Combine vinegar, garlic, ginger, salt, chili powder and cloves in saucepan. Add reserved mango syrup. Bring to boil; reduce heat. Simmer, uncovered, 30 minutes. Remove cheesecloth bag containing cloves. Add mangoes, raisins and sultanas. Bring to boil; reduce heat. Simmer, uncovered, 30 minutes more.

• Pour mixture into sterilized jars. Seal. Store in cool place.

Makes about 4 cups.

NOTE: Do not double recipe. Chutney will take too long to cook.

CUCUMBER RELISH

Pat Wood, mother of Toronto chef Bruce Wood, contributed this family favorite to a Mother's Day article I wrote in 1986 called "My Son the Chef." Wood claims that this was one of the few dishes her fussy son raved about when he was growing up. And I can see why. The recipe works best with your basic ordinary cucumber ("The kind that grew in our garden," says Wood) rather than the English kind.

12	large ripe cucumbers	12
6	large onions, peeled	6
½ cup	salt	125 mL
4 cups	white vinegar	1 L
½ cup	all-purpose flour	125 mL
3 cups	granulated sugar	750 mL
2 tsp	ground turmeric	10 mL
2 tbsp	celery seeds	25 mL
2 tbsp	dry mustard	25 mL
1 tsp	freshly ground black pepper	5 mL
½ cup	water	125 mL

• Chop cucumbers and onions coarsely in food processor. Place in bowl. Sprinkle with salt. Let sit 20 minutes. Drain.

• Combine cucumber mixture and vinegar in large heavy saucepan. Bring to boil. Boil, uncovered, 20 minutes.

• Combine remaining ingredients in bowl. Stir well to form smooth paste. Add to cucumber mixture. Bring mixture to boil; reduce heat. Simmer, uncovered, 5 minutes more.

• Pour relish into sterilized jars. Seal.

Makes about 16 cups/4 L.

GOOD-FOR-YOU GRANOLA

Storebought granola is often higher in oil and sugar than it needs to be. It's surprisingly easy to make your own healthier version. I offered this rendition, brimming with fibre and flavor, in "Breakfast of Champions" in the winter of 1987.

5 cups	quick-cooking (not instant) rolled oats	1.25 L
½ cup	wheat germ	125 mL
½ cup	natural bran	125 mL
1½ cups	sunflower seeds	375 mL
1½ cups	chopped walnuts, pecans, hazelnuts or almonds	375 mL

1 cup	unsweetened flaked coconut	250 mL
⅔ cup	honey	150 mL
½ cup	safflower, sunflower, soybean or corn oil	125 mL
2 tsp	vanilla	10 mL
1 cup	raisins	250 mL

- Preheat oven to 325°F/160°C.
- Combine all dry ingredients except raisins in large bowl. Mix well.
- Combine honey, oil and vanilla in small saucepan. Heat just until hot, stirring. Add to oats mixture. Mix well. Transfer mixture to two large shallow baking dishes or cookie sheets. Bake 25 to 30 minutes or until golden brown, stirring occasionally. Stir in raisins. Cool completely. Store in airtight containers.

Makes about 12 cups/3 L.

BARDI'S CHEESY GARLIC BREAD

Use white or orange Cheddar for this cheese-laden garlic bread from Bardi's Steak House in Toronto. It works best made with day-old French bread.

1	large wide loaf French bread	1
½ cup	butter (room temperature)	125 mL
1	clove garlic, minced	1
4 oz	old Cheddar cheese, grated	125 g
4 oz	mozzarella cheese, grated	125 g
3 tbsp	Cheez Whiz or other cheese spread	45 mL
½ cup	freshly grated Parmesan cheese	125 mL
2 tsp	butter (room temperature)	10 mL
½ tsp	powdered chicken soup base	2 mL

- Preheat broiler.
- Cut bread into 12 slices.
- Combine ½ cup/125 mL butter with garlic in bowl. Spread on one side of bread slices.
- Combine remaining ingredients in bowl or puree in food processor for smoother results. Spread mixture onto buttered side of bread slices.
- Place slices on cookie sheet.
- Broil until bubbly and browned. Cut each slice in half.

Makes 24 slices.

CHAMPAGNE FRUIT PUNCH

Go easy when you reach for yet another glass of this mouth-watering party punch. Laced with brandy and plenty of bubbly, it's likely to creep up on you and pack a punch before you know it!

1 cup	brandy, chilled	250 mL
4 cups	unsweetened fruit juice (strawberry, apricot, orange, peach, etc.), chilled	1 L
2	750-mL bottles dry Champagne or white sparkling wine, chilled	2
1 cup	fresh strawberries, halved	250 mL

• Combine brandy and fruit juice over ice cubes in large punch bowl. Gently add Champagne. Garnish with strawberries.

Serves 15 to 20.

FABULOUS FRUIT PUNCH

Eliminate the booze from this gorgeous, mint-laced punch prescription, and you've got a great non-alcoholic version.

1	48-oz/1.36-L can unsweetened pineapple juice	1
1 cup	sweetened orange juice	250 mL
¼ cup	fresh lime juice	50 mL
½ cup	fresh lemon juice	125 mL
⅓ cup	loosely packed fresh mint leaves	75 mL
1	375-mL bottle vodka or gin (optional)	1
1	750-mL bottle soda water	1
1 cup	fresh strawberries, halved	250 mL
1	unpeeled lemon, sliced	1
	Mint sprigs for garnish	

• Combine fruit juices and mint leaves in pitcher or plastic container. Refrigerate at least 2 hours. Strain mixture or remove mint leaves with slotted spoon. Pour into punch bowl over ice cubes. Pour in vodka. Stir to combine. Gently add soda water. Garnish with strawberries, lemon slices and mint sprigs.

Serves 20 to 25.

VAL'S SPARKLING ROSÉ PUNCH

Sun fashion editor, Valerie Gibson, gave me this recipe for her favorite party punch.

2 cups	unsweetened fruit juice (tropical fruit, pineapple, orange, etc.), chilled	500 mL
⅓ cup	fresh lime or lemon juice	75 mL
½ cup	gin	125 mL
1	750-mL bottle dry sparkling rosé wine, chilled	1
2	unpeeled limes, thinly sliced	2

- Combine fruit juice, lime juice and gin in large punch bowl over ice. Gently pour in wine. Garnish with lime slices.

Serves 10 to 12.

CHESTNUT STUFFING

My personal favorite at Christmas, Thanksgiving or any other excuse to roast a turkey. This recipe makes enough for a 14-lb/6-kg bird.

1½ lb	chestnuts	750 g
½ cup	butter	125 mL
2	large onions, finely chopped	2
4	stalks celery, finely chopped	4
2	medium carrots, finely chopped	2
½ tsp	dried marjoram	2 mL
2 tsp	dried sage	10 mL
2 tsp	dried thyme	10 mL
½ cup	unsweetened orange juice or chicken stock	125 mL
12 cups	stale bread cubes	3 L
	Salt and pepper to taste	

- To peel chestnuts, see page 54. Chop chestnuts.
- Heat butter in large heavy skillet or saucepan with lid over low heat. Add onions, celery, carrots, marjoram, sage and thyme. Cook, covered, 15 minutes or until vegetables are tender. Add chopped chestnuts. Cook, covered, 5 minutes more. Transfer to large bowl. Add juice. Cool completely. Add bread cubes. Toss lightly but thoroughly. Add salt and pepper. Chill until time to roast bird.

Makes 16 cups/4 L.

CORNBREAD STUFFING

An all-American way to dress up the festive fowl, this stuffing is superb and well worth the effort. This recipe makes enough to stuff a 14-lb/6-kg bird. Cook any leftover stuffing in a lightly buttered ovenproof dish, along with the bird.

½ cup	butter	125 mL
2	large onions, finely chopped	2
3	tart apples, cored and chopped	3
1 lb	bulk sausage meat	500 g
8 cups	coarsely crumbled cornbread (page 120)	2 L
3 cups	coarsely crumbled bread	750 mL
1½ tsp	dried thyme	7 mL
1½ tsp	dried sage	7 mL
⅓ cup	chopped fresh parsley	75 mL
1½ cups	chopped pecans	375 mL
1 cup	chicken stock	250 mL
	Salt and pepper to taste	

• Heat butter in heavy skillet with lid over low heat. Add onion. Cook, covered, about 15 minutes or until softened. Add apples. Cook, covered, 5 to 10 minutes or until apples are softened but not mushy. Transfer mixture to large bowl.

• Crumble sausage in skillet. Cook over medium-high heat until lightly browned. Drain off fat. Add sausage to onion mixture. Cool completely. Add remaining ingredients. Toss lightly but thoroughly. Chill until time to stuff and roast bird.

Makes about 16 cups/4 L.

INDEX